SURVIVAL OF A BLACK MAN:
AGAINST ALL ODDS

WELCOME TO SO-LOW

HARRY JOHNSON

SURVIVAL OF A BLACK MAN: AGAINST ALL ODDS WELCOME TO SO-LOW

iUniverse books may be ordered through booksellers or by contacting:

iUniverse
1663 Liberty Drive
Bloomington, IN 47403
www.iuniverse.com
844-349-9409

ISBN: 978-1-6632-5782-6 (sc)
ISBN: 978-1-6632-5783-3 (e)

Print information available on the last page.

iUniverse rev. date: 03/13/2024

INTRODUCTION

SO-LOW

This story is about a fictional Child Support Division set in a small California town approximately two hours from the Oakland, San Francisco Bay Area, called So-low.

So-Low reminded me of Petticoat Junction; Petticoat Junction was a television show that I use to watch as a child in the 60's and early 70's. It was a comedy that took place in an old country town full of white folks. It also has a large population of Mexicans because the out skirts of town consist of orchards, farmland for produce, horses, and liver stock. I asked a few Hispanic co-workers if they prefer being called Hispanic or Mexican because I did not want to offend them; most of them go by Mexican. The town was an old country town at that time it did not have all the fast-food joints, it only had MacDonald's, and Jack in the Box, on each end of town with a Taco Bell in the middle of town. It did not have a Target, Home Depot, or a mall. It did have a small shopping center that consisted of a very small Ross and JC Penney's. The center also had other small businesses, one of the businesses was a liquor store and a Mexican restaurant, the entire town was about thirty miles around, not counting all the farmlands that surrounded the county.

The town's nickname was the town of Trees because it had the more trees per capita than any town in the state; signs were posted at each end of town stating the fact. The first time I read those signs it sent chills up my spine and gave me an uneasy feeling; not because I was scared as I am not afraid of any man. Being born in 1960 in Berkeley and raised in Alameda, California which is the neighboring town to Oakland, you could not leave Alameda without going through Oakland.

I realized African Americans, white people and trees have an unhappy bond amongst each other after watching all the civil rights activities on television in the 60's and 70's. When I read the town signs, hangings was the first thing that crossed my mind; call me paranoid, but I am not the paranoid type either, my mother did not raise a fool, I did not make it to my sixties being a fool, but I am the cautious type, the type of person when in doubt I don't do, but I did not let the unhappy cautious thoughts stop me from completing my goal of getting this job.

I soon realized if any unhappy southern hospitalities were happening in California; they were happening in this area of California. The town had "good ole boy" written all over it. Everyone drove a Ford F150, Chevy or Dodge Ram truck; if you did not have a truck then you were not a Caucasian or a Mexican. There were thousands of trucks in the town; I was the only person in town who did not own at least one truck. Even the women drove trucks! I would sometimes see a woman drive into a gas station with a trailer of livestock hooked to her truck. Get out of the truck with her jeans, cowboy hat and boots to handle her business; some were fine looking, some not so fine looking.

The people who lived in this county believed in their 2nd amendment rights to bear arms and they did not care how many school children were shot up. They refuse to give their precious guns up for any reason; there was a lot of reddish color necks in this area. You got the message?

The town had a population of approximately sixty thousand people at the time; it is made up of about seventy percent white, twenty percent Mexican, and ten percent Asian, Indian, and African American. The white community runs about ninety percent of the businesses in town and in the county, the other ten percent are Mexican restaurants and other service type businesses like repair shops, gardening, and landscaping. There were also a couple small auto dealerships in town.

There is a large community of non-documented Mexicans in the town. President Chump would have a field day in So-Low as most of the illegals worked on the outskirts of town for the farmers receiving below poverty level wages and living in one or two trailers on the farmer's properties. They are six, seven or more deep in each trailer while the farmers and their families are living in their nice warm homes. Many farmers also paid the illegals under the table for taxes purposes; some of the famers would protect their illegal workers like they were their own children, they would sometime even pay their child support for them. Once an illegal is located by the CSD a wage assignment would be issued to them under their ID number at their place of employment. Some of the ID numbers would come up under someone else's name; most of the time it was either a deceased person, or they would not have a valid California driver's license. Sometimes they would have a fake ID number and card, or a number which did not exist in state records (this was a common practice). Because the Mexicans would need at least an ID to get a job, they would purchase a counterfeit ID. There is always a good counterfeiter in the low-income areas of the cities across the country; some of these copies are nice quality work.

This is a huge problem within the United States. The women of the United States would get pregnant by the illegal man and the man would go back to Mexico. The CSD most of the time would never be able to track the father down. After all, how many Jose's, Carlos's and Juan's do you think are in Mexico? The USA has what is known as reciprocity with certain countries. This means we could send the wage assignment to that country, and they would collect on the case on our behalf. These agreements are with countries who the USA have a good relationship with; I do not know how many of these countries we have a good relationship with; I would guess about three or four now while President Chump is in office. If the CSD is unable to locate the father; then guess who will have to pay for that child? You and me. Especially if the child is receiving some type of family assistance, aid, or welfare. Which is all the same; whatever you want to call it.

Bob, California is also located in So-Low. The townies look at people from Bob California as snobby, uppity! With good reason because Bob is a town that has the University of California at Bob (UCB) is located. The residents of Bob tend to be lawyers, doctors, business owners and other highly paid professionals. Bob is a cool town to enjoy drinks and dinner; the town has plenty of small restaurants and bars. It is a college town on one side of highway and on the other side of the highway it is a respectable residential area where you can raise a family, nice parks, dog parks, jogging and hiking trails.

Townies are poorer financially and is more of a red-neck personality, Duck Dynasty type of people, good old boys. You can go to a bar to have a drink after work or later in the evening and there is a good chance of you will run into a drunk white boy trying to get in a fight. Cowboy hats: guys too busy drinking to dance with their girlfriends. You are going to see a lot of this as you continue to read this story.

This story all started in late 1999; Bill Clinton was the President of the United States. He was in office when we qualified to buy our first home. He is also recognized as one of our first Black President for some things he did while in office for the people of color. He was not the first President who tried to help Black people; but he did help blacks make progress both negative and positive. He was one of the first presidents who cared about the Black people and made presidential moves to try to give Black people a chance to prosper and buy their own homes. Clinton was like Kennedy, Obama and Carter; he concentrated on closing the racial gap between different racial groups. His policies and initiatives brought greater hope to the Black community and other nationalities. He got my vote when I saw him on the Arsenio Hall Show, I thought to myself, anybody who can play the saxophone like he did. Must be cool! So, he got my vote. He also had sense enough to admit he made a mistake when he signed the Violent Crime Control and Law Enforcement Act of 1994. That law provided billions of dollars to build privately owned prisons in the USA to house more inmates. This caused mass incarceration of mostly Black and Brown skin individuals, inmates had to serve eighty-five percentage of their sentence before possible release. More money for the increase in police officers across the country and the mandatory three strike rule which is basically a mandatory life sentence, the bill also had a clause stating the government had to keep the prisons always populated with inmates.

This story is about a middle-aged Black man from the inner city of Oakland, Alameda, located in Alameda County applying for a job with the County of So Low and being hired. He did not know this area at all, he had never been in this area of the state other than when he was passing through on the way to college. Even then he did not actually drive through the town, he had never heard of Tree-land in California.

My family and I purchased our first home in a town called Fairfield, California. Fairfield is more of a city without the rat race and crime of the inner city. It is located forty-five minutes north of Oakland, and San Francisco and forty-five minutes south of Sacramento. Basically, the suburbs for these three larger inner cities. My family consisted of my wife and my two young children, a seven-year-old boy, and a three-year-old girl. I was working at a law firm in Oakland and my wife worked for a mortgage company in the city of Walnut Creek, California. After purchasing and moving into our home we soon realize we both worked on the opposite side of two bridges; with our kids attending school on the other side of both bridges in Fairfield, my wife and I decided I would work my job until I found another position with another company on the Fairfield side of the bridge. My job did not offer medical coverage and her job did; that made it easy for us to decide who was going to have to look for another position. We each made over eighty thousand a year at our jobs, so I started looking for another position with another company. It took approximately three months to locate the position with So-Low. I then resigned my position with the law firm at Jack London Square in Oakland.

I accepted the position as a Child Support Officer within the So-Low County District Attorney Office in late 1999. I was proud to get this job because it seemed to be a rewarding position helping all the kids and single parents in the county. Not all the parents lived in So-low; some were in other cities, counties, states, and countries, but their cases originated in So-Low. It was also rewarding because my mother had just passed away in April of 1999; because of her I always had a soft spot in my heart for single parents as I lived her struggles as a single parent. I had four older siblings to help her with me since I was the baby of the family; my two oldest siblings', a brother, and a sister, was raising their own family at this time in my childhood.

I was offered the position because I was qualified. I was overqualified as I came in with about 25 years of accounts receivable experience, both legal and straight collection experience. I was interviewed by three white women, one somewhat professionally dressed, the other two dressed good enough to go to the park or for a casual Friday. It was not Friday; I was dressed for success with my pin stripe dark blue suit white freshly pressed collared shirt and a purple Nordstrom professional looking tie that I sometime wore on special occasions. I did not have any problems communicating with the three women supervisors, and I was offered the position with a one-two vote, not to hire me. "Yeah," that is what I said! Not to hire me! One of the supervisors Pam, she was the only supervisor who wanted to keep me. She was the professionally dressed supervisor; one out of the three supervisors wanting to offer me the job, I thought it was funny since I knew I could handle the position. I was offered the job even though the other two supervisors (with the same first name of Sarah) did not want to offer me the position at least that is what Pam told me after I decided to accept the position. I passed all the background checks and was bonded and given an oath which I was to obey and live by the law of the land. The oath included my responsibility to report any abuse, wrongful act or unlawful incident that involves a child or elderly person, or any crime committed that I might witness. I must pledge to report these unlawful incidents to the police immediately or be prosecuted and sentenced to up to five-year imprisonment. That did not scare me because that is what I thought any normal person in their right mind would do. I could not be out there getting into fights, getting a DUI and getting arrested, these negative acts was ground for an automatic termination for a person in my position.

I started the position with So-Low County Child Support Division in September of 1999. It was actually a part of the District Attorney's Office at that time and all new employees had to complete a one-year probation period. I started working for So-Low despite the so low salary they offered me; I took a significant pay cut for this position. I wanted to turn them down, my wife and I talked about it, and she persuaded me into accepting the job because of the medical plan that came along with my position. The financial offer was a slap in the face, it really insulted me. The medical plan was better than my wife's medical plan at her job. They offered a good medical and dental plan for my family and a good retirement plan through PERS; so, I accepted the position with the So-Low County District Attorney's Office Child Support Division.

I soon found out I was working in a County in California that was as racist as you can get; it took me exactly one day and a couple hours to come to this conclusion. Coming from the Oakland-San Francisco Bay Area it was hard for me to understand that I would run into racism like this so close to the Bay Area. Call me naïve! I knew racism could raise its ugly head anywhere and at any time; but have these people ever heard of a feeling out period? Or a getting to know a person for a period before you start with the insults. No! Not these country assholes, they start the shit slinging almost before I walked through the door. Not everyone in the department was pot-ty trained; not everyone had respect for the different races, creeds, or religions. There were just some low-down dirty people who simply enjoyed pushing the little power they had on others, both male and female. All supervisor and management positions were held by white people; there was one Mexican women in the HR department who completed my hiring. She was a nice older woman who was due to retire a couple years after I started, but for the rest of management that meant I could not hit any of those knuckleheads upside their heads for at least one year. Believe me, in my mind, I was slapping the shit out of a lot of them, and this was my first day on the job.

Within my first week on the job, I met an attorney, he was a white middle age man; he thought he would feel me out with racial jokes every day. If the joke was not racial, it would be religious or vulgar in nature. I believe he was testing my temperament; all the other employees would overhear his jokes and would wait to see how I would react or respond. This was very troubling to me as I had to waste my time to straighten this out during my first week or two of employment. This idiot, continued with the jokes during my first two weeks before I decided I heard enough, I had hoped he would stop on his own, but I soon figured out I would be waiting quite a while for him to do so. One time he approached me with another racial joke that had a punchline which included my mother. I looked him in the eyes and said if he told me one more racial joke, I would take him outside to the parking lot and whoop his sorry ass. I told him this quietly and man to man. He is white male in his low to mid fifty's, he looked at me in my eyes and realized he finally crossed the finish line with me. I always say when fighting, may the best man win and may you come in second! He worked in the department for another year before he was transferred to another division after he sexually harassed one of the white women in the office. Upper management did not react to an incident unless it affected a white employee. He asked a female coworker "if this reminded her of something", then he proceeded to open his mouth and display a wad mashed potato. No, he was not fired, just transferred to another division. He was transferred to the criminal division so he can get unfair sentences for the minorities being prosecuted in So-Low. I was just glad the asshole was gone because I was not going to take any more of his shit, I am not a violent person, I usually give a person three strikes to fuck with me, then I stop the stupidity. Let me put it this way, I am Gemini. I have a real good side and I also have a real bad side; I usually let the other person choose which side they want to deal with. I am prejudice, I am prejudice against assholes, I do not care what nationality you happen to be, either you are an asshole or you're not.

I soon realized that I had plenty of other attitudes to deal with. The office was like ninety percent women mostly Hispanic and white women. There was one black woman in the office. She was there for a very short period after I arrived. I believe she was terminated when she left the office. I was mad because she had borrowed five dollars from me a week prior to her departure, I never received my loan back. That was the first time I had ever worked in an office that did not have any Blacks other than myself, all my other jobs were in the Bay Area where diversity reigned in every employment office.

After going to lunch for the first couple of months. I soon realized

I was one of about three African American men in the entire town; the other two African American gentlemen were in the Child Support System. They may not have been living in the town. Just had babies that were conceived in So-Low. I would see the same two black gentlemen at a fast-food restaurant, driving, and sometimes at the bus stop. They would also come into the CSD occasionally; they were never together, so I do not believe they knew each other. There were about the same amount of African American women I would see around town; but I was not sure if they lived in the town, I would see African American women far and few between.

Call me naïve again, but it was hard for me to believe a town existed this close to the Bay Area and was this racist. But I was wrong; racism is right down the street from the Bay Area. Oakland has a reputation that proceeds itself; there is a certain respect that goes along with the city of Oakland, this respect and reputation is known all over the world, I am not saying there is no racism in the city of Oakland, but at least they have sense enough not to say it out loud. The city of Oakland represents a large part of Alameda County. Alameda County consists of a large racial mixture of people like Blacks, White, Hispanic, Asians people from all walks of life, sexual preference, and cultures from all over the world living together like a can of mixed nuts.

In So-Low they had White and Hispanic and that was it as I continue my employment, I continue to experience different situations that did not sit well with me. Being a somewhat religious man with a strong religious background and base, I soon realized this county had a telephone prefix of six-six-six this made me feel uneasy and it also help explain a lot of the negative vibes. I am somewhat superstition but not to the point I walk around the poles on the streets; I also would not walk under a ladder. But six-six-six is the devil and I personally do not want to have anything to do with the devil, I hated calling these numbers, but I did because of my religious belief. I worked with a lot of devils both male and female; I use to wonder was this hell on earth because with the six-six-six prefix and how hot it got in this area of California each summer. It rained hard in the winter and felt like hell right here on earth in the summers. I like heat, but this heat is up there with Arizona heat almost, but not as dry. It would get up to about one hundred to one hundred and eight degrees, which was hot to me. I thought Fairfield was hot, but out there it gets at least five degrees hotter. It never got that hot in the bay area because of the cool ocean breeze that blew constantly off the Pacific Ocean.

BETTY

On my first day of work, I met this little old white lady name Betty; she looked in her late sixty when I met her, she oversaw all the files, if you need a file or could not locate a file, Betty will locate the file and bring it to you. I felt bad for her; she would be pushing the little cart with the files in it and struggling while she was walking, her knees would be pointed inward, they was almost touching, her walk would get worse by the days, she had a curvature of her spine and was pigeon toed, she would almost be looking at her feet while walking, but this old woman was one of the strongest and stubborn woman I had ever seen in my life.

Betty's favorite team was the San Francisco Giants, she loved her some baseball and the Giants. I told her I was an Oakland A's fan; she said, she feels sorry for me, she would always walk around the office with her Giants baseball earrings on and have her little transistor radio in her cart. She would be walking around with her little wire running up to her ear listening to her Giants games. She knew the players and their batting average and other statistics.

I asked Betty did she ever think about retiring; she said when I retire it will be time for her to die. I said wouldn't you like to just kick back at home; she said I am the type of person who like to do things, she does not like just sitting around doing nothing unless she is watching a Giants game. She said working makes her feel young and useful; I could not argue with that, when I first met Betty, she looked at me like she did not like me. She said that is because she did not like my ass! I said, why you did not like me; she said, because you are black, I looked at her and she looked at me and she started cracking up, I started laughing because she started to laugh, she was a wise ass also!

Her health was failing, and her legs was in bad shape; I would ask her if I could help her; she would make a head lock with her arm and tell me to come stick my head in it; she said, she always gets one more mile out of her legs. Betty had three adult kids, she had out lived three of her prior husbands, she use to say her second husband was the most fun, but he was no good; her third husband was the one who left her with the most money; number one husband was the one she loved the most, she is an older woman with a strong and solid sole that is the reason why she was fighting death and winning; she told me this one day. Giving death a run for its money, fought dead with both tooth and nails; that is the reason why she got up each morning and went to work; she had over a hundred vacation days and sick time paled up. After about two years of working with Betty her legs really started giving out on her, she started pushing her cart sideways and was leaning on the cart, I do not know why management continue to let her push the cart, the last three months was terrible watching her suffer; one day she did not show up to work. Everyone had a feeling something was wrong; we found out that day she was rushed to hospital in the middle of the night. We found out she was in her early eighties; her legs had finally given out and she was not going to get one more mile out of them. Unfortunately about three weeks later she passed away, a lot of my co-workers did not know I went to visited her in the So-Low Hospital; we talked during the visited she told me in a very faint voice she was a racist at one time, when she was younger; she was taught not to talk to blacks or hang out with them; and she could not go in a blacks family's home. She had one black family that lived on the corner of her block; her parents would not allow her to go in their home even though they played together every day. She said her second husband had black friends; she really got to know them, and they helped her figured out that her parents were lien to her all this time; she said Harry it was a pleasure meeting you, she said your mother did a good

2

job raising you. She said she is not doing well; she does not believe she will be going home again, I told her I will pray for her; she may be going home to the Lord Jesus Christ; she said that will be better than going to her home; Betty said bullshit! We started laughing one last time together. She ended up passing away a few days later. She was a nice old woman with an even better spirit. I was blessed to meet her and have her in my life; she was a good person. Whenever you meet a good person with a good heart, they are a blessing rather you recognize it or not.

DRIVING WHILE BLACK

One morning early in my employment; I was driving to work, I would take highway five zero seven which is a two-lane highway in each direction; it is a highway built on the out skirts of town; it normally flowed smooth when it came to traffic, I would take this highway and it would connect to another smaller one lane highway nineteen. This particular morning I was rolling to work and I was the third car in a line of four cars we all was traveling about two car links apart; the posted speed limited was fourth five miles per hour; all four cars was traveling at approximately fifty-five mile per hour; we past a highway patrol car traveling in the opposite direction, all four cars continue to travel pass the highway patrol officer and paid no attention to him, all four drivers felt comfortable while passing the officer, no one hit their brakes to slow their vehicle. I looked in my side view mirror and I saw the officer turn on his lights and started to turn around in the middle of the highway, after he passed about three more vehicles, I really did not pay attention to him, because I thought maybe he received another call that made him turn around. As the officer was racing up the highway in the same direction with his lights flashing the cars behind me started pulling over to let him pass by them, I pulled over so he can pass me, he pulled over behind me and stopped, the cars behind me drove off. I'm thinking, why did he pull behind me? The officer was getting out of his car, and I got out of my car and asked why did you pull me over? He unsnapped his gun guard on his holster and put his hand on his gun and yelled at me to get back in my car! I said oh you going to shoot me now! I said again, why did you pull me over? The two cars ahead me drove off, he picked my car out of all four cars. I was the only Black driver out of the

4

four cars that was pulled over, I was not the last car of the four cars, I was third in the line; I got back in my car after he told me for the second time to get back in my car with his hand on his gun; I asked why did he pull me over; he said because you was speeding; I said all four cars was traveling together at the same speed; he said he clock me going faster than the other three vehicle; I started to laugh and told him you lien, he asked for my license, proof of insurance and registration papers, I gave him all the requested documents he went back to his car and everything checked out, when he returned I told him he pick me out of all the cars to harass me; I told him to give me the ticket so I can go to work, he took his time walking back to his car, played like he was writing the ticket again, he took his time writing the ticket to make me later then I already was, when he returned to my car; I told him I am on your side, I work for the DA Child Support Division, I am on your side, I took the ticket and got ready to drive off; I told him I should raise your child support, we looked at each other and I drove off! I called him a racist asshole! "I said that to myself"! I told Pam my supervisor about what happen to me on the way to work because I walked in late. Later on, that day Pam received an email from the officer stating I threaten him; when I told him I should raise his child support. Pam asked me if I threaten to raise his child support, I told her first I did not know if he had a case in our office, we searched his name on Pam's computer system and he did indeed have a case in our office. I told her yeah, I told him I should raise his child support, I told her, I also called him a sorry motherfucker when I was driving off, "I said that to myself", she made me write the racist officer a letter of apology or he can get me terminated since; I was still on my one-year probation. I wrote the letter for one reason and one reason only for my family, I had been working for about six months at this time. I was mad; because that asshole officer who was a white boy racially profiled me and went out of his way to

5

harass me; he saw I was black man; it was a clear morning; he turned around in the middle of a highway to give me a ticket; that is how bad he wants to give me a ticket.

I never forgot the officer's name; his ex-wife called a few years later and the officer came in our office; I am not sure if he recognized me, but I recognized him for sure, I never forgot his last name, because I had to write him the letter of apology. We cannot just change your child support to what we want, we must obey and follow the state and federal laws of the country, that still leave officers plenty of room to bend your ass over and fuck the shit out of you, with no grease. We raised his child support, So-Low raise that racist cop child support about eight hundred more dollars a month for one child, he had a second family who he was supporting, he had three children but only two kids were his biological kids, he wasn't obligated to pay for the third child. He was not happy when he left our office. I really think he recognized me, but I was not sure, that is what is meant by "what goes around comes around;" when it came around; I fucked that racist cop in his ass like an uncircumcised African. The bible said the Lord works in mysterious ways, he was pissed when he left our office; not only was his booty hurting, but his wallet was also. I usually do not seek revenge; but that was too easy and there is one thing I cannot stand is racism; I guess it's because it's always happening to me. I have run into racism all my life, elementary school, high school, and college. Racism is a part of every black man's life, if you have not run into racism then you are not a Black in America.

NO MORE PIZZA

There was a lady who was a few years older than I; she was hired a few months after I was hired. Her name is Carol, she was a tall and somewhat heavy-set woman and lived in town. She was married and hired as a temp employee. She was a nice woman; mother of about four kids who was older, I believe one of her children had a couple children at a young age. She and husband were like all good parents helping to raise their grandkids. Our friendship picked up quickly because she like to talk shit and so did I. She was proud of her town and heritage, she also loved her local professional team the Sacramento Kings, they was not season ticket holders but went to the games quite often. We would bet lunch when the Lakers and the Kings would play in the playoffs or during the season, the Lakers would always win the series and most games during the season, I never bought lunch, but I respected her loyalty for her team.

She liked telling me about how her brothers made her and her sister tough, she stated she broke three guy's noses in three different fist fight; I believe she was protecting her brothers in two of the fights; she would walk up on me and say, "what you going to do Harry?" She would be looking eye to eye with me; I would look at her and say nothing! "We would both start cracking up laughing!" I used to tell my co-workers I would fight her, "but she is bigger me!" I said this behind her back; I use to tell her, I was going to manager her in the WWF, I told her I can get her in a cage match against Hulk Hogan for the championship belt winner take all, she said the Hulk cannot handle her in the ring or anywhere else, I would say I believe you Carol my money is on you.

We started going to lunch together a lot because I was not familiar with the town at all, we became somewhat good friends, but not in a sexual or courting way, we were just friends and co-workers. She was being nice to me because she realized I was out of my element; it was strictly platonic relationship. We would go to different restaurants and have lunch; majority of the time we went to Man Mountain Mike Pizza and ate all you can eat pizza and salad; we would pay for our own meals, I do not believe the town had a Roundtable at this time, it also had a couple privately own pizza joints, but no Shakey's Pizza or Roundtable.

This lasted for approximately a month, one day Carol and I was going to lunch but she left without me; the next day she had something to do, I was starting to get the feeling something had gone wrong; so I asked her why she did not want to go to lunch any longer, she told me her husband was a police officer in town; his co-workers would see me riding in their cars; she drove most of the time, because she knew the town; her husband's co-workers would go back and tell him they seen his wife riding and having lunch with a Black man. I am going to say Black man instead of the word "nigger," because I am not a nigger! But we all know which words the good ole boys chose. I could somewhat understand where he was coming from, I wouldn't want my wife going to lunch with another man every day; I would not care what nationality he happen to be; we never went to lunch together again from that point on; other than department lunches; we worker together for years, we continue to be good friends at work, she was someone I like to calling a five a day week friend, she was a republican all her life; so white is right, I use to tell her right is right, I am sure she is MAGA supporter and probably donate to his campaign; might even showed up to a couple of his rallies with no mask; this would not surprise me at all, but the majority of white people in town consider themselves republicans and the majority of them do not have republicans money, most of the families in town was lower income or on some type of assistance; they do not give a damn about diversity or helping anybody out side of themselves, the rich getting richer and the poor getting poorer this would be just fine with them, white is right, my ass! Let's move on!

SLEEPING UGLY

Bob was another person you will get to know during my first five years of employment with So-Low, he was an older Hispanic man who worked there before I was hired, he was in his late fifties or early sixties, he had retire from a prior job with another company. The only problem with Bob; he had a serious problem staying awake in his office, this use to be funny, you would walk pass his office, he will be hunched over his desk and key board in the seating position; eyes closed, and sleeping with the door wide open; you could hear him snoring sometime; It was one of the funnies things I had ever seen in an office environment, everyone in the office including supervisors and managers knew of him sleeping on the job; this was an everyday occurrence; he would say he was praying as a joke, he was Catholic but he did not attend church every Sunday, well no Sunday's, he was watching the games on Sunday mornings. I will never forget when I walked in his office and he had fell asleep with his finger still resting on the (R) key; his screen was covered with the letter (R), he woke up and realized I was standing over him and he said Amen! I said Bob, you know dam well you were not praying, and we cracked up; he continued to sleep in his office for another two years before he retired without any of the supervisors or managers disturbing his time of rest. He used to walk in late every morning, even later then I, he lived in town, and I drove about forty-five minutes to work. He knew I was a good cover for him; they were so busy trying to catch me in something, he got away with murder when it came to him sleeping. The only thing he was missing was his jammies with the feet in them; his blanket and pillow; he was never written up or disciplined for him being unconsciousness four to six hours a day. I do not think he has sleep apnea, he told me he would have what he called a "pop" or two every night, I said every night, he said it would put him to sleep at night, he said that was his warm milk at night, I said do it put you to sleep in the bed with your wife or in your big recliner in front of his TV; see he use to brag to me about his big recliner, he said it depend on if he has a third "pop", I said whiskey would sing rock-a-by-baby to you each night, he said yeah, and we cracked up but he was good man deep down inside, he would help you if you needed it.

NAAACP AND PAM

Pam is another character that you will need to know about in my story. She is a white woman who was well off financially through her family; she and her husband were also well off from their work history; her father was independently wealthy she was brought up with a sliver spoon in her mouth; poverty was not a word in her vocabulary, she did not deal with people of color daily; only when she had too. I believe she grew up in the wealthy area of Southern California; she did not know how to deal with people of color or seen people addicted to drugs other than on TV; this was a large percentage of the people we dealt with in So Low; she looked down on people who was poor and less fortunate than she.

I remember one time she asked me about the NAACP. She said Harry what does the NAAACP mean? I said first it is the NAACP, and it stands for the National Associate for Advancement of Colored People. I told her it is an organization created to protect people of color from the unlawful acts that has occurred in the USA, political, socially, educationally, economic equality and to eliminate racial discrimination and to assure all rights for all people.

I asked her one time if she knew who the actor Denzel Washington was, she did not know who he was! That told me she did not watch movies with Black people in them; Denzel Washington is one of the top Black actors in the movie industry, he has starred in movies with other well-known white actors and actresses; there is no way she should have not known who Denzel was, she either grow up on another planet or all blacks looked a like to her, I even pulled up a picture of him and she still did not recognized him.

I started working on the second floor at the beginning with So-Low; during the first year of my employment they started a new unit called PST, which stood for the Public Service Team, this was created to help people and co-workers with quick fix issues; like people walking in with questions and issues that could be rectified in a fairly quick manner; we would discuss their case or cases and give them the necessary documents they would need to rectify their situation. Pam was named the supervisor of PST, she asked me to go down to PST and work in her department, I asked her will I still have my own office downstairs? She told me no, I was going to have to share an office with one other co-worker, I told her I rather stay upstairs in my own office, then to go downstairs and share an office, after all I still really did not know anyone, and I already had negative experiences in the first few months I worked there.

She kept insisting it would be best for me to go down stairs to PST, she kept telling me she would take care of me, she kept telling me the two other supervisors did not want me, she kept stating I was still on probation, because my year was not completely up, she kept promising me she would take care of me, so I decided to accept her offer and go to PST and work under her supervision, I share an office with Carol first, we got along pretty well for the first six months and then she moved to one of the other double offices in the department with this lady name Mary, Mary was a little older then I, she was a white woman who was married to a Hispanic gentlemen who had a bad knees and he worked around her parent's farm, they lived on her parent's property.

I had this other white woman move in to my office; she came from upstairs, she was a season veteran in the CSD, she was an older woman who stood almost six feet and weighted over two hundred pounces, she was a former police officer, she told me when she first moved into our office she was not scared of me, she stated you may intimidate the other employees; but I did not intimidate her, she stood up and looked me eye

13

to eye when she said this to me. I was thinking to myself, "bitch"! I will beat the shit out of you. As we became office mates; she realize I was not a threat to her, she realized I was not going to try to kick her ass, she loosened up with me and decided to tell me somethings about herself, like she was a nudes, she stated she went to different nudes camps around the state of California, she particularly likes Stinson Beach in San Francisco, she thought it was nice, clean and well operated, it was also a reasonable travel distance for her, she would go by herself, with a boyfriend or with a group of friends, she stated she did not wear clothes around her home, she just like being naked, she would say, she was born that way, God could not be wrong, I use to say "Amen"! She would laugh, she said I feel so free when I am naked, she stated she always wore the least amount of clothes as possible; that explained why she never wore a bra or panties, she was a big woman and older, she was in her late fifty's at this time, the reason I knew she either did not wear panties or wore a thong, she like wearing those big flimsy dresses which hung loose on her, her dress would creep in to her ass crack when she walked around the office, It was not like I was making it appoint to look, but you could not help but see it with her big ass, she had. It was not big and pretty, it was just there, if you know what I mean? I used to tell her she did not want to cook bacon, fry chicken or fish why she was walking around the house naked, I also use to ask her if she closed her curtains while walking around her home, she said sometimes. I asked if she could come to work naked, would she? She said hell yeah, she would welcome the opportunity to come to work butt naked. Sometimes she would walk by and I would ask her if she smell fish, she did not know what I was saying, sometime when a woman vagina get an infection of some kind it will give off a fishy smell, I was just saying it because she never wore panties.

We became cool; she would help me if I needed it, she took me

14

under her wing, she start to treat me like I was her little brother, which I appreciated because at the time I need as much help as possible, she was like a child support encyclopedia for me, she taught me a lot about the child support rules and regulations, you can easily be overwhelmed with the work. She was a nice older white woman; I appreciate her assistance; we were office mates for a couple years.

I had a third office mate another white woman; she was a nice woman who was a season veteran in the child support field, she was little gullible and somewhat of nice lady. She loved her dog; her dog was a bulldog; you know one of those short pudgy dogs with the pushed in face bulldog with the two bottom teeth sticking out of their mouth. One time she moved from one home to another, and her dog was having a problem adjusting to the new environment; it was shitting everywhere, she would go home at lunch to check on him and he would have shit all over her new home, she could not leave him outside because it was too hot outside, and he would die from heat stroke. So, she asked Pam if she could bring the dog to work with her; there was only one problem they never considered asking me what I thought since she was sharing an office with me. You know white people love their dogs more then they love their relatives; she brought her dog in for about two months. This was not the first time I share an office with a dog, because some of the people I had worked in the past was doggish in one way or another, but it was the first time I had shared an office with a real dog. I cannot remember his name; I called him Archie Bunker because he looked like Archie Bunker, this dog had more gas than Chevron, and I did not think the dog like Black people because he would not fart until I walked in the office. All my co-workers thought it was funny, I would walk in the office and five minutes later I would have to walk out of the office. He even took a shit on my side of the office before I arrive to work one day; Rose was cleaning up the last bit of the shit when I

15

walked in the office one morning. I was going to report the dog, but I knew the white people probably would have fired my ass, before they got rid of Archie Bunker. Rose eventually found someone to take care of her dog during the day while we were at work, she end up retiring from the CSD, I believe she moved up north to Oregon or Washington to live; and no, they never gave a damn about asking me if it was ok to have the dog share my office. I wanted to slap the shit out of them for sticking that dog in our office, I love dogs like the next person, but not in a place of business, unless it is a service dog, not because a dog may have the flu and cannot stop shitting on himself. I say prop him up on the toilet and leave his ass at home, don't bring him to work and have him fucking with me, I can see the animal cruelty people coming after me right now, let me quit while I am behind! Next!

DIFFERENT TYPE OF ANIMAL

Child Support is a different type of animal; it is nothing you can learn overnight; it is a profession that will take at least two to three years before you will start feeling comfortable with the workload. There are so many ways a child support case can turn, every person who come through the door is different, there's no two cases alike. If you could imagine all the negative things that go on in people's homes across this country; physical and mental abuse by men, women and children, molestation of men women and children, drug use in the home, women testing dirty and baby testing dirty at birth, child being taken from the mother five minutes after child is received in this world, children abandon at any age or time of day or night, men saying he does not want to pay the mother, a women scorned, she has it out to ruin the man's life one way or another, men that did not wear protection and get the woman pregnant the first time they have intercourse in the back seat of the car, in the woods, in a bathroom where ever you can imagine having sex or not imagine having sex, It only takes one time, believe it, because it is TRUE! Women who use the rhythm method for birth control; you know what they call men and women who use the rhythm method for birth control? Parents! Men and women straight out of prison, some men come out of prison and had never seen their child, some women come out of prison and have not seen their child for the last five years or more, women having their child while incarcerated, man get a STD while the woman gets pregnant during intercourse, I'm trying to help men and women get a job; and you can find their picture on Megan's Law, sexual offenders who father children, incest between two relatives and they produce a child. Every day I went to work, I never knew what I might hear or see that day.

17

Child Support turns ugly the moment you step out of your home and into my office; I would not wish this on my worst enemy, like the great blues singer Johnny Taylor say "It is Cheaper to keeper her"; the day you step out your home, it is one of the worst decisions you have made in your life, the Federal Government and State Government will hold you accountable for that child or children, every agency who work with the State and Federal Government will pursue you to the point of no return; every month you miss a payment, every license you have with the state will be suspended, then when you make a payment the state will reinstate all your license until you miss another payment, your driver's license, contractor's license, insurance license, real estate license, fishing license and barbers license, any license with the state and every month you miss a payment, they levy bank accounts, all of them, liens on property, have you served and brought into court, issued wage assignment, intercept taxes both state and federal, intercept stimulus checks, the state will take twenty five percent of your unemployment check, passport shut down and incarceration is also on the table. This is just some of the things that will happen to you, none of them you will want to write home to your mother about.

People who walked into PST department to be helped and was assisted by me, always wanted to talk to me from that point on, they would come in and ask for me, or would ask for the Black man when they could not remember my name, they would want to deal with me only. My co-workers told me I had rock star status; I would treat all the clients with respect, and they wanted to deal with me only, I did not talk down to people or disrespect them, some of my co-workers would sometime treat their clients disrespectfully, give their clients plans to pay their on-going child support and arrears back that was not going to get their account current, or a plan that was not realistic for the non-custodial parent to maintain, they did not care about the mother, father, or the children, they gave them pay back plans that was going to fail from the moment they walked out of office, I am talking about giving a person who is struggling financially a plan that was going to be impossible to pay back, they might be working on a farm, or making less then minimum wage, or a person who has not been working at all, they would give them one hundred or two hundred dollar payments they know when the client left the office they was not going to make the payment consistently or for twelve months, some may not be able to make the payment the following month.

We was lucky if illegals would stay in the country or at the same address we had on record for them; you will call the Non-Custodial parent he or she will play like he does not speak English or say we have the wrong number, Illegals may not have a driver's license, just ID card they purchased when they entered the country under the table; counterfeiters, some of these counterfeit ID's would have information for a person who had passed away, they would have his Hispanic name transferred to the card. The dead person's info would be the info of an American who passed away ten-twenty years ago, when we checked the numbers three different names might come up under that number, I am talking about people who has been dead for ten or twenty years. They had a number of excuses they used to beat the system; some of the parents should not have been in the country in the first place, they could have gotten in trouble in the country from a past visit and should not have been able to cross back into the country, because they was kicked out of the country or did not have the proper work papers to return, some illegal women will get pregnant in the USA or any other country and the baby is born in the USA, the baby is automatically a US citizen but the parents are not US citizen, this is known as an Anchor Baby when the mother and father is an illegal and the baby is born in the USA, this will open up avenues for the parent to get citizenship much easier and quicker.

The terrible part of having an illegal as a father is they can leave country and we will never be able to locate them; since we were not able to locate the father that means the child will grow up as an American citizen not knowing his or her father, this could damage the kid to the point the child will never get over not knowing where he or she come from, never knowing their Grandparents and other family members, this could effect this child for their entire life and through their early mental and physical development, it could cause depression, or other mental issues which can follow child into the adult stages of his or her life, now this child is twenty years older and considered an adult, when deep down inside this person is thirteen mentally, now this depressed young man or woman has to deal with the law in this cold and cruel world we live in, this is never a good thing because the outcome is undetermined and unpredictable, then these individual become parents themselves and it starts the cycle all over again, I saw this first hand as a Child Support Officer. Some of those kids saw me as their daddy; I helped support them, I saw them from childhood to adulthood, I also saw some get locked up, and others go to college it is not all a terrible ending there are some success stories, but the success stories did not come easy for these young adults.

You would be surprised at how many women have a baby with illegals; especially, the Mexican women, they are Roman Catholics, they do not believe in birth control that is the reason you see Mexican women and men standing in front of Planned Parenthood Offices across the country. I heard Mexican women has an average of four children; I do not know if this is true, but in my twenty years of employment in the CSD I have seen hundreds of Mexican women walk in the office with multiple children. When I say multiple children; I am talking about more than two, I also heard that statistic on more than one occasion within the CSD, I am not knocking Mexican families, I believe to each his own, this is just facts or fiction I learned during my years on the battlefield in the CSD. Remember I was in a predominately Mexican and White area and office; I remember one time I went to lunch and I saw this Mexican young lady with four kids, she could not have been older then twenty-four years old, I came back into the office and went to my Mexican co-worker Bob and I asked him why every time I walk out of this office I see a young Mexican women with more than one child? He confirms what I heard, he stated Mexicans are Roman Catholics and they do not believe in birth control, I told him thanks for confirming what I heard, I will make sure I stay far away from them, one thing I did not want is some more children.

I also realized I could not have a relationship with any women who walked into my office or any other CSD; if I laid up with them I better not be looking at their account, or assisting them with their case, that would be automatic termination, if one of those custodial parents would have gotten mad at me, that would have been an automatic termination for me, I know a former co-worker, white boy that got busted for fooling around with a custodial parent and he got transferred to another division of the county, I would not have received the same treatment, they would have fired my ass without a doubt, that is called White Privilege, So-Low was dishing out white privilege like government cheese.

That is enough of an introduction to So Low County, let's move forward to the real crap; you may not believe what you are about to read, but I will be writing all these events to the best of my knowledge and my recollection, also remember all this shit happen to me, so no one remember the beating like I do, we are talking about twenty years of racism, and other crap, so please enjoy the read but do not enjoy my agony too much! The characters in this book is fiction.

FIVE WOMEN AND A KNUCKLEHEAD

This happen after about a six to nine months on the job, the county sent about twelve employees to a training in South Lake Tahoe; it was nice, each employee had their own room in the hotel with a built in Jacuzzi Tub, our husband and wives could come for the four days, but my wife was working and could not take the time off for the trip. Everyone had the choice to drive in their own vehicles or we can ride in the county van; the van did not have the county name on the side of it, it was just a white van with bench seats and carried about twelve to fifteen people, I was going to drive up by myself, but they needed someone to drive the older women up to the lake, they asked me to drive the van, I was like "all shit", I do not want to drive these women up to Tahoe. There was only five of them riding in the van; two people dropped out of the van when they found out I was driving, I did not care, it did not bother me at all, the morning we left for the trip there was three older women Teresa, Sandy and Rona that was riding in the van, a young white girl Sandra and a Black girl name Rhonda. I drove to work and left my car in the So-Low parking lot. I loaded up everyone's luggage in the van and everyone climbed in; we started out on the three-hour drive from So-Low to South Lake Tahoe. We jumped on the freeway and was rolling smooth, some of them was sleep, the young white girl Sandra stated awake during the ride, I told them if anyone needs to use the restroom, just let me know, I will get off the freeway. They said OK, if they get hungry, we can eat. I was just driving for about an hour; Teresa woke up and said we should start thinking about using the restroom and grabbing something to eat. I said OK. So, we start to go through this little town located off highway fifty; I asked them where do they want to eat? I said McDonald's, Burger King.

Teresa said in her elegant voice "ole no we must sit down and eat" we do not eat fast food; she said we must go to a restaurant and sit down to eat; we must let our food digest properly. Teresa was an older woman in her early to mid-sixties, she had worked for the county about thirty years, she was due to retire in the next year or two, she was a beautiful older Hispanic woman, still fine, wore a lot of nice expensive jewelry, always wore her makeup nice, she had crow's feet around her eyes but still a nice-looking woman for over sixty.

Sandy was also a nice-looking older woman who I believe was Italian; she was being forced out, not because she cannot handle the work any longer, she refuses to use a computer, she had worked on paper for so long it was difficult for her to adjust to the computer. She had about thirty years on the job also, she was another older woman that cared about her appearance, always had her makeup on nice, had her rings on her fingers; she and Teresa was good friend outside the office also. Sandy was acting in the small theatres in Bob California; there was some performance art studios arounds the campus in Sacramento, Berkeley, and the San Francisco Bay area. She really enjoyed performing in front of people; she had worked with a lot of promising actors over her years in the small theatre, I did not really get to know them until the trip, it was really the first time I got to know everyone in the van except the young black lady she worked in Public Service Team with me.

Rona was Hispanic woman in her mid to late fifties she was a nice woman heavy set; I had to keep giving her extra help getting in and out of the van, she would step on the floor board of the van and the van would lean down on one side of the van, it was funny. Sandra the younger white woman would act like she was in an earthquake while Rona had her back to us and trying to get on the back bench seat of the

23

van, she would be in the back snoring. She was a nice woman; she had a problem with her legs, and she was just working to try to get a five-year work pension added to a prior retirement. I told the young white girl she was not right for making fun of Rona. We smiled at each other, and she said she was sorry.

Sandra started calling me Hope from Driving Miss Daisy; because of the three older women I was driving, she was a nice looking young lady with a good personality and a nice smile, she was a single parent who was in the child support system, they all worked upstairs, she said her boyfriend was going to drive up in a couple days and stay with her the last day and night, she said she might not ride back with us, she was younger then I by approximately ten years, she was in her mid-twenties, I told her as long as she make it home ok, that is all I care about, she said she will be fine, he is a good guy.

I asked them what they wanted to eat; Teresa said is there a sit-down restaurant, I pulled in this little restaurant parking lot, we all walked in, this white lady was the waitress that walked by us a couple times and on her third pass she said we can sit anywhere. Teresa got mad; and said did you hear what she said, I said yeah, she told us to sit anywhere. Teresa said no Harry; she should stop and look at us, then direct us to where we are to be seated. Teresa and Sandy said they was not going to eat here if she cannot treat us with respect; so, we all walked out of the restaurant, I helped Rona back in the van and I drove about two blocks, we saw a Carrols Restaurant, so we decided to go in there and eat. Carrols restaurants always had a good reputation so we went there; we ate and talked for about two hours, that meal turned our three hour trip into a five hours trip, I was driving but the older women was the boss, they were calling all the shots, we left at nine a/m that morning, we should had been arriving at twelve noon, but with this two hour breakfast slash lunch we had push the trip from three hours to five

24

hours, then the older women started asking me did I have to use the restroom, Rona would say, I know you have to go to the bathroom, every man who is a real man has to go take a shit after they eat breakfast, she said that is a known fact. I said I did not have to use the bathroom, Rona said OK, let wait a little while he will need to go, I really needed to go handle my business, I thought about holding it, since they were talking about it, it gave me a perfect opportunity to handle my business, Teresa said we are not going anywhere until Harry go to the bathroom. Sandra the young white girl said Hope will you go take a shit; so, we can get the hell out of here, Rhonda said yeah please Hope go take a shit! I grabbed the newspaper and went on my way to handle my business, we all started cracking up, I figured I better stay in there and read the paper for a while incase Rona did not like my time limit. When I returned to the table Sandra started clapping and barking like a dog, and yelling Hope, Hope, Hope! I told Sandra; I was going kick her ass before the trip was over. We all started laughing they paid the bill while I was in the restroom, they said I did not have to pay for any food while we were traveling, they all agreed to cover my meals since I was doing all the driving. I told them thank you. We went back to the van and I helped Rona get in the van; yeah the van lower when she stepped on the running floor board, I looked at Sandra sitting in the front passenger seat while Rona was making her way back to the rear bench seat in the van, I looked at her like don't act like it is an earthquake, she did the motion real slow, I just smiled and laughed a little bit, closed the side sliding door and walked around to the driver's side and got ready to hit the road. We still had about two hours to travel so before we reached South Lake Tahoe; I cut the radio on, and we listen to music and mosey on down the road. We got about thirty miles outside of South Lake Tahoe; Rona say I have to use the restroom, I said Rona a real woman would have use the restroom at Carrols, she said I did use the restroom,

25

so I pulled over at Shell gas station, Teresa said Harry you do expect us to use the restroom at a gas station, let's find a restaurant so I drove down the street and it was a Shari's restaurant, I pulled in the lot, we all got out, I helped Rona out of the van and yeah it lowered down when she stepped on the running floor board and again, Sandra played like it was an earthquake. We all used the restroom; I helped Rona back into the van, yeah when I helped Rona back into the van, Sandra act like it was an earthquake and we got on down the road. Approximately forty-five minutes later we were driving into South Lake Tahoe. The hotel was a nice ski lodge, and everyone got their own room with a Jacuzzi tub in each room. Sandra was excited about the hotel; she was from Tree-land and had a couple kids, she was not making enough money where she can take her kids and have them stay in a Hilton or Embassy Suites hotels, she really enjoyed the luxury and the nice TV's, I told her she better not touch the mini-bar, she said don't worry, I have already checked the prices. Everyone except Rona spent the day walking in the little bit of snow that was still stuck to the ground, It was still a lot of snow, but not enough to cover the roads to the point we needed snow chains, it was some beautiful scenery both walking around and from our hotel rooms, It would get down to about thirty degrees overnight and got up to about fifty during the day, our classes was held in our hotel, so we did not have to leave out in the cold, Rona spent the day in front of the fireplace with her hot toddies, Rona was cool, and funny, she would sit in one of the best seats in the bar area with the fireplace and take her shoes off to have her bare feet next to the fire getting warm, she would said I am making my feet nice and toasty. Sandra said to me her feet does not look like toast, then I said they look more like Texas toast, or two canned hams with toes, then I said I hope none of her corns pop on her feet, Sandra and I was cracking up, a little later we went back to our rooms after having dinner and a couple drinks.

26

The next morning everyone got up, got dressed and had breakfast together, we went to the conference and completed the required steps necessary to complete conference. We were schedule to depart the next morning, so that night we all partied together. We had dinner, drinks, and partied pretty late that night, Sandra boyfriend called her and told her that he was not going to make it up, he stated he had to work late, Sandra was pretty bomb out because he could not come up for the night, so she got pretty drunk that night, she started saying she was going to kick his ass, she would ask me if I think he is messing around on her, the more drinks the more she asked me if he is fooling around, I told her I do not know her old man so I cannot make that call. I told her that is why they call if fooling around, because he would be a fool to mess around on her, Sandra said you are right, he would be a fool, she was starting to get drunk, I told her, she needs to slow down on drinking. She asks me if I wanted to have a drink with her in her room. I told her Hope does not want to mess around with her, I told her you know I am married, Sandra said she will not know, I told her I will know, she cooled out after that, I told Sandra, do not let someone turn her into something she's not. Teresa, Sandy, Rhonda, Sandra, and I continue to talk with Rona having drinks, appetizers and listen to some music. It was a cool rest of the evening after we helped Sandra back to her room, the ladies help her into bed, while I walked back to my room.

The next morning, we slept in and met in the lobby at about eleven-thirty, check out time was at twelve. I helped Rona in the van and Sandra played like she was in an earthquake, we laughed, Sandra said her head was hurting from the night before, she said I had how many drinks? I told her about five, about three different liquors, she said I know. Sandra asked me if I would mine her going to sleep while I am driving home. I told her I will give her a pass. Rhonda was tired also because she drunk enough to have a hungover, so she was also sleeping, let me just put it this way Hope was the only one who was awake on the way back, even Teresa and Sandy were both sleeping. When we got about two hours down the road, they all started waking up and had to use the restroom, I was enjoying my piece of mind, listening to my music while they were asleep. Sandra woke up first, I started looking for a diner so they can use the restroom. We decide to stop at the same Carrols Restaurant. 'Yeah', we spent another two hours having lunch, I did not have to go to the restroom so that saved us another half hour. Yeah, I helped Rona back in the van, and she walked to the back of the van, Sandra shook like an earthquake again and we got in the van and rolled on back to the office and got in our own cars. Sandra was going to kill her boyfriend when she got home, she was also happy to see her kids. Sandra and I worked together for another five years before she decided to leave So-Low and go work in Sacramento with another company. She was cool, I enjoyed working with her during our time together, she never married her boyfriend, I was glad she did not marry him, I met his sorry ass one day he was biker, grease hair, and was basically trying to live off her. We talked one day in my office when she came down to see me, I told her he is no good, he was about ten years older, I asked did he have any money? She said no, I asked her does his parents have any money? She said no they do not have any money. I told her to get rid of his ass. I told her what my dad used to tell me "Dead weight broke the wagon down!" I told her she was fine enough that she would not be on the market long. I believe she took my advice and split up with him. I believe he had her co-sign for him a car before he left, we had one of our attorneys in the office to draft him a letter and he brought it back, she had to get a voluntary repo for the vehicle before she moved on, but she left his ass.

Teresa she worked with me for about another three years then she put in for retirement; she lived in town her husband had passed away, she had her daughter and grandkids living with her, I would sometime see her in the office when she stopped by to visit and to say hi, she would always stop by my office to say hi, and talk about our trip to Tahoe, she said the trip was one of the highlights of her worked career, she always talked about how much we laughed on the trip. She said she loved when Rona was talking about me going to the restroom; and I was driving three Miss Daisy's, she said that was so funny, and she would say what was your name Harry, I said Hope, she would say yes and started cracking up. It did not bother me, I knew she was sincere with her questions, I love Teresa she was a cool older woman.

Sandy continues to refuse to use the computer for the most part; she continued acting at the small theater around the area, she also retired approximately the same time as Teresa. I heard Sandy passed away a couple years after she retired; she lived alone, I heard her daughter lived in Boston, she would visit her from time to time. Sandy was a nice lady, I really enjoyed knowing her, I never got the opportunity to see her perform, I read a couple of her performance reviews that she had posted on her wall in her office, the reviews was all positive reviews for her and the cast. I was sorry to hear that she passed because she had a good heart.

Rona retired about five years after the trip, she was one of our receptionists; she had real bad knees partly because of her weight, she was also a nice lady, she and Rhonda was the only two people in the van that I had talk to prior to the trip. She was a lady who liked to smile and laugh. She had a couple of adult kids; that was approximately my age or just a few years younger, when she retired, she was living with her sister somewhere.

Rhonda was cool until she heard I was writing a book of poetry and suddenly, she wanted to write a book of poetry, she also wanted to use a similar title, she was younger than I, she borrowed five dollars from me and ended up leaving, I believe she was terminated. I do not remember why she was terminated, but maybe she quit. I still like her even though she owed me five dollars, look like I came out on the short end of all her shit, but it is cool, I shook it off. That is what happen on the great five women and a knucklehead business trip, I really enjoyed that trip, it was good personalities, and good attitudes riding together no one got on each other nerves. Thanks to the Lord.

LESLIE

I also had a good friend name Leslie; she worked on the public service team with me, she is Mexican young lady that was cool and she was fine also, Leslie was older and she was one of the more stylist representatives in the office, she was also a single mother of about four kids, she had four different baby daddies, all her kids was getting up in age, two of her children was already over the age of eighteen and two kids considered minors, her youngest was about nine. Leslie was about forty at the time.

After my family and I moved in our first home for about two years; I had been on the job for almost two years, I threw a house warming party at my home, I invited about six ladies to my home from work, only two co-workers came to my party one was Leslie and the other was an attorney that had just started with our office, she started approximately year after me. She brought a girlfriend with her to the party; they brought tequila and drink mix with them, they also brought some beauty to the party because my friends were all trying to talk to them during the party, they were fine and classy, I already had beautiful women at my party, but you never have enough beautiful women at your party.

Leslie came to my party; she brought her brother with her; he had done some prison time and had a couple of children in the child support system already. Leslie had been running the streets a lot more than the attorney and her friend. The Attorney and her friend came from money. Leslie did not have money; she was a single parent, had been married and divorce a couple of times. She was a strong Mexican woman that has been rode hard and put away wet. She was older than our Attorney and her friend; she would also not have a problem whooping another woman or man's ass if she had too.

One time we had these men on probation and parole working in our office; they was changing the lights in the entire office and doing other work around the office, Leslie started to like one of them, she started talking to him, she like showing her stuff with her low cut blouse and her short miniskirts, she had a nice figure and she made a lot of heads turn, including mine, she look good walking around the office, she knew exactly what she was doing. She pulls out the flirting device; she uses to call it, you know the smiling and laughing to sucker him in, she would look at me and say Harry watch me sucker him in, I use to say suck that sucker in, and we would laugh.

Leslie started going out with him until he decided to put his hands on her; she picked the guys that like putting their hands on her, she would walk in bruised up after a couple weekends, she did not have problem telling them motherfuckers off, she would curse them out on the phone all the time, some time she would curse them out in Spanish. I would not understand a word she was saying but I knew she was cursing them out. I told her a man is a motherfucker if he hit a woman, she said there is a lot of motherfuckers out there. She had been beat by almost all her lovers; she told me Mexican men like controlling their women and they do not have a problem beating their women. I said every Mexican man; she said nine out of ten of them would hit their wife and their kids, I said kids need they ass whooped some time, she said this motherfucker hit the wrong woman, because he is going back to prison for hitting her, all she had to do is go back to her desk, bring up the county directory, she can fine his probation or parole officer in one or two calls, that is what she did and he was on his way back for another two to ten years stretch depending on what his prior offences

32

happen to be, it could be longer depending on if he is sitting on a third strike, he could not get out at all, inmates call it bye, bye, momma!

She was a cool co-worker to talk too; because she had live life, she had done a little traveling, club and bars scene around the Sacramento and Oakland, San Francisco Bay Area, she was a funny older woman, she had no problem talking shit and having fun. She smoked marijuana sometimes, but had a drink probably every day, and could dance her ass off, could do all the latest steps.

She ended up losing her job approximately a year later after; she had been employed for about twelve years, she started working for the county a few years after she graduated high school. She was off ill from work for a few days; she was trying to help her brother with his child support case from home, instead of waiting until she returned to work to check our system, she decided to try to call me to get some info for her brother. When she called me, I was not at my desk; she decided to call another representative name Karen answer the phone, Leslie thought Karen was cooler than she was and asked her for the information concerning her brother. Karen told the supervisor Pam; it is a cardinal sin to work a case of a relative or friend, this is automatic termination in the office, Leslie ended up getting terminated soon after talking to Karen, Karen knew exactly what she was doing when she told on her. She knew she was going to be fired; our calls was not recorded so Karen had to snitch on Leslie, I was surprise she snitched on Leslie, I also thought Karen was cooler then she was, that just proves that you never actually know a person, like you may think you do, I was somewhat mad at Karen for snitching on Leslie, she knew Leslie's living situation with her kids and she went on and had her terminated anyways, to me you do not do people that way, she could have just told her she need to do that herself. Yes, Leslie knew she could get terminated by her actions, I have this saying sometimes "I am surrounded by stupidity". I thought it was stupid on Karen's end and Leslie's end. That is what I meant by that saying.

A lot of woman in the office was jealous of Leslie; Leslie knew how to turn a man's head, she had a good personality and a pretty smile, jealousy was her down fall, I hated to see her go because I considered her a good friend in the office, Leslie would have never done any of her co-workers like she was done, she wanted to whoop Karen's ass, I always kept my guard up around Karen from that point forward, six months after Leslie was terminated I never heard from her again, I believe she still lived in town. I heard she had found another job in Sacramento, she continued to raise her remaining children. Leslie was cool in my book, and I missed her after she was gone.

JONNY: SABOTAGED

Jonny was a young lady who started working as a temp; she worked for approximately a year as assistant to all the officers working on PST, she was a white woman that was approximately thirty- five to forty years old, looked like what the older generation would categorize as rode hard and put away wet, could be considered basically white trash. Skin dry, hair oily, and had a couple children and divorced, and her living situation was hit and miss, she was feisty and would give you a good tongue lashing if you pissed her off. I thought we had a pretty good work relationship; she continue to work there for about a year and decided to apply for a permanent position as child support assistant, she ask me to put in a good word for her with our manager Pam, she knew Pam and I had a pretty good work relationship, I spoke to Pam on her behalf, Pam was considering offering Jonny the child support assistance position anyways, Pam was glad that I spoke to her about Jonny, I just help reassure her decision. Pam offered her the job and Jonny was glad to have it; I was glad for Johnny because she had her two kids to take care of and I knew this would help her quite a bit.

Jonny turned into an entirely different person after she was hired; she started talking back to the officers including me when we asked her to do her job, she was having problems with our receptionist, they had been working there longer then she had been, she was arguing with me and the rest of the officers, I remember one time I asked her to do something for me, she told me to do it myself, she did not have the time to do it today, I asked her at ten in the morning, she did not take it, she also started missing work days. She started talking back to Pam; debating with officers over how they were handling their cases, all the other officers came into my office, told me they chose me to go talk to Pam about Jonny and her behavior since she gotten hire. I talk to Pam; I told her Jonny is going crazy, Pam said she knows, she already had rubbed Pam the wrong way a couple of times, Pam said she hope Jonny does not forget she is on probation for a year even though she had worked as a temporary employee for over a year.

Jonny then tried to Sabotage one of my cases; I gave her a file with all the necessary child support documents in it, the documents was held down by a two-hold punch clamped down at the top. A child support file holds all original documents that was completed and sign by the non-custodial and custodial parents; all court orders judgements, photos of parties involved, man, woman and child or children, all documents are also scanned to our computers. I asked her to finish preparing some documents; I need to serve and have the non-custodial parent sign documents on our next schedule appointment. The morning of the appointment came; I needed the file, suddenly, the documents I had prepared and gave to her to complete was no longer in the file. When I asked her for the file to deal with my client on his next visit and to sign the documents; she stated I never asked her to complete the documents, I said you do not remember me asking you to complete the documents I had prepared, she stated I was lying and mistaken about asking her to complete the documents. The legal documents I asked her to complete was documents I did not have the knowledge to complete and was not my job to complete. Child Support Assistance had the knowledge to complete the documents; and was trained to complete the legal documents. I had been employed about three years at this time; Jonny was still on her probation, my co-workers and I was suspecting Jonny was using drugs again; some time she smelt like alcohol also, her odd behavior also gave her away. I had the file prepared and had the necessary documents completed and signed by our attorney, the non-custodial parent was able to wait for the documents. I was able to serve him and have him sign all the necessary intake documents. Jonny was very upset at me; she said I was trying to get her fired, about an hour later this Mexican female co-worker named Rhonda came to me and said she heard me asked Jonny to complete the documents for my client, Jonny was in a cubicle, Rhonda sat on the other side of the wall, she stated my voice travel, she heard me giving Jonny specific instructions on what I needed. Rhonda reported what she heard to our manager Pam; Pam called Jonny into her office, when Jonny left Pam's office she was pissed, she was cursing, cutting her eyes at me and my other co-workers, she had Rhonda afraid to exit the office. After Jonny left the office Pam went through her desk; she located my documents, I also had notated my computer stating I asked Jonny to complete the necessary documents. Jonny walked in the office the following morning; everyone could tell she had a bad night; her attitude was terrible, she was ready to jump down any body's throat who approached her, most employee stayed away from her. Pam was talking to the director of the division about terminating her; I did not care, deep down inside I wanted her terminated, she did not give a dam about me and my family, I continued to work there for one reason and that was to support my family, that was the only reason why I took this shit from my co-workers, I had to keep my job for my family. In this very short time of employment, I had been racially insulted by the lead attorney; had a co-worker try to sabotage my work, I had only been employed for approximately two years, maybe a little longer.

Pam ended up terminating Jonny; she was raising hell while leaving the office, she was cursing and slamming stuff at her desk, she grabbed her coat and other personal goods, started walking out, she stopped by my office and told me I was fucked up, said this entire division is fucked up. I said bye "bitch"! "I said that to myself"! I know she was calling me a nigger deep down inside, but she never said the word out allowed, which surprise me, she left the office.

Jonny continue to go on a downward spiral with her life; I heard she was drunk at the county fair, had a fight with someone, and was arrested. I thought I seen her at a stored one day a few months after her termination, I believe we both played like we did not see each other, I am sure she did not want to approach me outside of the office with her nonsense, she made the right decision I would not had been so nice to her, I would not have hit her, I do not hit women, but knocking her ass out might have cross my mind a couple times, if you know what I mean, I never seen her again after that day, which was ok with me. I hate when I help someone make progress in their life; they end up turning against me as soon as they get what they want, this make a person not want to help others in their lives, because of the trust factor. I told myself; I was not going to put myself in that situation again; everyone for themselves for now on, that was about the third time that happen to me, three strikes and you are out, it will not happen to me again.

SO-LOW FAIRGROUNDS

Every summer So-Low would host their annual county fair; it is the only fair in the state of California that still had free admission, we had one Mexican supervisor at this time name Carla, she was a nice woman, she always treated me nice, she was from East Los Angeles and lived in Bob, California. She was married in her early to mid-fifties; she approached me one day and asked me, if I want to work with her at the fair, she stated she observed me with my clients and she felt I would be a good representative to work with her at the fair in the CSD booth, I told her no thank you, I do not think this would be a good ideal for me to work at the county fair, I would be working during work hours in the afternoon. I told Carla; no thanks you, I do not think this is a good ideal for the second time, she said look Harry you can get out of this office from about one (PM) to four-thirty (PM), she said it is a beautiful day, we will be at the fair, she stated all I have to do is pass out pamphlets and trinkets toys to the kids, I will also have to talk to some non-custodial and custodial parents who may have questions and pass out a few business cards, she said it will be an easy, and relaxing. I liked Carla she was cool, she was not like some of the other women in the office; she was from the city, so I told her I would go to the fair and hang out. We drove in her car to the County Fairgrounds it was only about ten miles away. Once we started working the booth it was nice; the booth was in a shaded area, the afternoon was going good for about an hour, I was handing out trinkets to the kids and answering questions while talking to the parents.

This little white girl walked up to me; I asked her if she want a trinket, I reached down to hand the trinket to the little girl, her

39

grandmother turned around right when I was handing the trinket to the little girl, her grandmother yelled "NIGGER" get away from my granddaughter! She snatched the trinket out of her granddaughter hand, threw it on the ground, I backed up and put my hands up in the air like the police had me at gun point, I did not want this lady talking about I tried to touch her granddaughter in the wrong way or anything like that!

The booth was made up of two wooden horses with two pieces of plywood laying across the wooden horses; Carla saw the entire incident, she jumped up and slid over the table, she told the old white woman not to talk to me like that! Carla said Harry; is a good man, father, and child support officer. We had our Child Support shirts on at the county fair, Carla had gotten me another Child Support shirt to wear to the fair that day. Carla said he did absolutely nothing to your granddaughter except give her a toy; he did not deserve you calling him that word, she told the old lady to get out of our section before she call the police on her, I just stood there with my hands over my head, if anyone was going to jail, it was going to be me, I was the only Black person in the entire fairgrounds at this time, I was probably the only African American that step foot in So-Low Fairgrounds the entire three or four days of the fair. I been a young Black man in America since the early sixties; I am an older black man in America today, there was one thing I did during these years of life, "I paid attention" to what is going on in this country; it cannot be my country while my people are being treated the way we are treated. If Carla would not had seen this incident there was a good chance, I would have spent that wonderful day in jail. There was other white's and Mexican's who I believe witness the incident, they might have stood up for me, I don't know. I would not have bet on someone standing up for me. What do you think?

Carla apologized for what the old lady said to me; I was in shock, there was a lot of white and Mexican around, I just went and sat down in one of the chairs on the other side of the table, with my hands still up. I told Carla; see I told you; I should not have come down here, the people out here in this town are stupid and racist, that is why I did not want to come down to the fairgrounds. Carla said I am so sorry that this happen to you Harry; Carla was starting to tear-up while she was telling me this, I told her that is alright Carla, I gave her a hug, you did not know that this woman was going to say something like that. Carla said that stupid bitch! She said, I should kick that bitch ass! Remember Carla was from East Los Angeles, she would have kicked that bitch ass. I said Carla then you would be going to jail with me. We both started laughing, we continue to work at the fair for another couple of hours. When we was on our way back to the office; Carla said she was sorry again; I told her that is alright, that is not the first time I ran in to a piece of shit like her, every time I drive into this town I expect shit like that, I told her every white household in this town have a grandmother like that woman, I said there is a lot of our co-workers would not go to lunch with me, afraid they might be seen with a Black man. I would have treated them better than their boyfriend or husband. Tammy was the only white woman in the office who dated Black man, she had all the Black movie stars, entertainers and pro athlete on her wall along with her black boyfriend, but she was not from the town, Carla was aware of Tammy and her Black boyfriends. I told Carla we are not going to let this ruin our day; we still had a good time out there; we passed out a lot of business cards to help the parents and kids. The next morning Carla came over to my office to make sure I was still doing alright; I laughed and told her I was fine, no damage done here, I really wanted to whoop that "old bitch ass" deep down inside. I said that to "myself"!

WHY CAN'T I CALL YOU NIGGER?

About a year later the State of California had their 50th year anniversary for the CSD; the state had a huge celebration in Palm Springs, California. All 58 counties were invited to the state of California CSD celebration; all managers, supervisors were invited, each Supervisor could invite one of their employees to go to the celebration, the celebration was for a week and all employees had their own rooms. Everyone from my office flew to Palm Springs because of the travel distance; some counties flew, some counties were bused in, some employees drove, everyone was reimbursed for all travel expenses, it was a good week.

We had to attend Classes and Seminar's during the week. There was also a dinner and a formal dance set up during latter part of the week; there was a few evenings where you were free to do what you wanted, like go to bars in town, the movies theaters, and shopping. Pam was my supervisor at the time in PST; she was the manager that was going to have to choose which employee was going on the trip with them, she had been going to lunch with Carol every day for the last two years consistently, so everyone in our department knew who she was going to take with her on the trip.

Pam called a meeting to announce who she decided to take with her on the trip; about ten of us was in the meeting, I was just leaning back in my chair waiting for the announcement to be made, everybody knew she was going to pick Carol, including Carol, she was probably already packed for the trip. Pam stood up; she said the person I decided to take on the trip to Palm Springs is Harry Johnson; I almost fell out of my chair. I said what the! I said to my other nine co-workers, she picked "Lil ole me"! I could not believe it.

One reason I could not believe it; approximately two weeks before Pam made her announcement to take me, I had been a bad car accident on the same two lane highway I always took on the way home from work, and the same highway I received the speeding ticket, It was highway nineteen a two lane highway, one in each direction, the highway had high grass growing from the farm lands that was all around the roads, it was dry grass; as I was coming around the bend, there was old man trying to make a left hand turn on to the road, he was to my right, as I was coming toward him, I saw him look left toward me, he then look right to check the cars coming in the lane he was turning in, but he made a cardinal sin by not looking left again, he started to pull out in front of me, so I checked the oncoming traffic lane and it was clear; I move into the lane to my left hoping that the old gentlemen would see me and stop in my original lane, I was traveling about fifty mph, he did not see me, and continued to drive like he was on a Sunday drive right out in front of me, I hit my horn and jammed on my brakes and yelled Ohhhhhhh shiiittttttttt!; and smashed into him! It scared the shit out of me! My front end hit him on his left quarter panel, he was driving a Lincoln Town Car and I was driving a Mazda Protégé, My car drove his car into a drainage ditch around this farm land, the ditch had about three feet of water in it, I ended up leaning over in the passenger seat when I finally came to a complete stop, good thing I had my seat belts on, or else I am sure I would have flown out of the car and probably died on the highway, when I was able to lean back up in my car and straighten out my glasses. I saw the old man in his car; water was starting to enter his car, I got out of my car while my back, knees, neck and every other part of my body was killing me, I climb down in the drainage ditch and grabbed his door knob and opened his door and attempt to try to pull him out, but my body was killing me, that is when this white lady appeared, she was in the first car driving toward us, she stated she seen everything, she said he

43

pulled out in front of you, she saw I tried to avoid the accident, she told me to go sit down, she will get the old man out of the car. So, I climb out of the ditch, and she pulled the old man out, the old gentleman kept say he was "so sorry sir", I am "so sorry sir"! I am "so-so sorry sir"! The ambulance arrives about ten minutes after the accident, they laid me on the gurney and took me to the So-Low hospital my car was a total loss. I had the ambulance medics to pull my brief case out of my car. When I reached the hospital; I was in some serious pain; I had bruises all over my chest, rib area, arms and waist area from the seat belt straps. I was out of work for about ten days after the accident, the Police officer who took the accident report told me at the hospital the man driving the Lincoln Town Car was ninety-two years old; he stated he should not have been driving in the first place. I said he never did see me coming, I tried my best to avoid him, but the closer I got to him, the closer he got to me, he never saw me, I thought I was dead. I told the officer thanks; he told me he would have the accident report for me tomorrow. I believe the only thing that saved my life beside the seat belts was that I worked out on a consistence bases and what little muscle structure I had help absorb the punishment that was inflicted to my body. I had to go to the doctor several times and had to see a chiropractor for about 3-6 months. I was torn up from the floor up!

When Pam asked me to go; I turned her down, she continued insisting that I go, she would say Palm Springs is the perfect place to go to rest, I turned her down at least three times, she continued to say no you are going with me. So finally, I gave in and told her I will go on the trip, I told my wife that Pam is refusing to take no for an answer. By the time we were to leave I was still in a lot of pain and was still on strong medication for the pain I was enduring, the doctor had me on Vicodin and Percocet to deal with my pain, so I was feeling good on the airplane and in my hotel room.

When we arrived in Palm Springs, I soon realized why Pam insisted on me going to Palm Spring, she would come up to my room every night to check on me and to try to have sex with me, I told her I was married, and she would say so am I! She would want to rub my back, I would let her until she started wanting to continually go lower on me, a couple of time we had to have a tug of war with my drawls! She trying to get my drawls down and I am trying to keep them up. I used to laugh; that was the first time a brother tried to keep my drawls on, usually I would be trying to take them off. I liked her as a person at the beginning, I might have laid up with her, but I was married and she was an older white woman with health problems herself, she had Diabetes really bad to the point she had an insulin pump attached to her waist, she would manually pump it in herself or the machine would keep track of her sugar level and automatically make the necessary insulin adjustments.

One night we was talking about having sex and she said Harry if we are making love and I look her in her eyes and her eyes roll to the top of her head where I will be seeing just the whites of her eyes, she told me to go to the sink, get a glass of water, come back and sprinkle some water on her face, she said that would revive her, that would snap her out of the coma she's in, I asked her have she ever been with a black man? She said no! I told her it was going to be a given that her eyes will roll to the top of her head, I then told her, let me make sure I understood her correctly. I said when I make your eyes roll to the top of your head, you want me to get off you and go over to my sink and get a glass of water and come over to you and Christian her by sprinkling water on her face to snap her out of the dick coma, she said yes, sprinkle some water on her face, she will snap out of the dick coma. I said are you "crazy"? I told her do you know what the law will do to me if she does not snap out of the dick coma! What they will do to me if they fine a dead white

45

woman in my room! I told her, they will throw me up under the jail, and throw away the key. She said don't worry; I will snap out of the dick coma. I have this saying I like to say in situations like this one. I like to say, "You might have choked Artie"! "But you are not going to choke Harry"! That simply means I am not going to fall for that shit! No way, shape, or form. It is not going to happen. She continues to try to get me to give in, But, I did not!

If I was not married; she was younger and not sick, I was not on all the medication, and not in constant and intense pain, who knows? Maybe, but in my current situation I was not going to step out of bounds, we all know men are vulnerable sometimes or all the time, especially when their family or wife is not around, but I left her alone, it was my best move for me at the time, I always go with the best move for me.

During the latter part of the week, I believe it was Thursday night we had our formal dinner and dance; I was not dancing too much because of the pain I was in, I was sitting at a table with Pam and Connie this Mexican assistant Supervisor. Connie transferred from another county; I said come on Connie and Pam lets go sit outside by pool, I will buy us a drink at the poolside bar, it was a beautiful night, and I did not want to dance. We could still hear the music at the poolside bar, and see everyone in the dance, they said OK, so we walked outside, and I bought the three of us a drinks. While we were sitting by the pool, Pam said Harry can I ask you a question? I said yeah, go ahead, she said now please do not get mad at me, I said to myself, aww shit! What is this woman going to ask me? She said promise me you will not get mad. I said OK, I promise. Connie and I looked at each other out the corner of our eyes because Connie knew Pam and she knew Pam might say something stupid. Pam said, why can black people, call each other the N word, and white people cannot! I told her first; I do not like anyone calling me the N word. I said but Pam if you want you want to call me the N word then go ahead; I will give you one shot, I give you one pass, if it would make you happy. She said no; I do not want to call you the N word, I said Go ahead! It is Ok! Go ahead! Connie was sitting there with her face in her hands, like what an idiot! Connie said why you must ask him this question; I told Connie no! Let me answer her question. I said Pam; I know you can call a white woman a bitch, or a whore and she might not jump on you; but if I called a white woman a cunt! Most white woman will jump on me for sure. Right? Pam and Connie said right! I said but what if Connie called you a cunt; would you get mad or would you laugh it off, she would laugh it off. Connie said Harry that is a great analogy! I said again I do not like anyone calling me the N word. So please do not call me it!

We flew home the next morning; after she tried to lay up with me again, then about a month later Pam was looking for an assistant supervisor, I felt I was ready to be at least an assistant supervisor so I applied for the position, Pam also encouraged me to go for the promotion, I had to interview with Pam and the Director of the CSD his name was Tim in the director's office. I went and interviewed for the position; I had been there for a few years at this time, they interviewed me for almost two hours, I never had any problems communicating with managers and other stiff shirts, when I left, I felt I had a good interview, I felt I had a good chance of getting the position. They asked me to have Carol come up to interview; when I got downstairs, I walked to Carol office and told her it is her time to interview and good luck. She walked down to Pam's office and Pam was not in her office, so Carol walked to my office and said Harry, Pam is not in her office, I said no, I told her she must interview in Tim office upstairs, Carol face turned a beet red color, I said what is wrong? She said we must interview in Tim's office, I said yes. I told her go up there and interview, I said do not be scared, you will be fine, good luck. Carol walked up to Tim's office; she returned to our department about ten minutes later, literally, she was crying, went home for the rest of the week, I believe we interview on a Wednesday, the following week on Monday I was called into Pam's office at about four o'clock p/m. Pam told me that she would have given me the position if I would have laid up with her; but since I turned her down, she was not going to give me the position, she promoted Carol to the assistant supervisor position. Carol was my assistance supervisor for the next year. I was mad, I wanted to file a complaint, but it was her word against my word, it would not have made a difference, in So Low they might have laughed at me, there was no way I was going to receive any support from any of my co-worker or the county. Pam used to always call me in her office; she would ask me to close the door; she would ask me to rub her shoulders from time to time because of her diabetes, I would do it sometime and some time I would not. Most of the time I would not. Ron another Mexican co-worked who worker in PST with me; he used to ask me, why do Pam always ask you to come to her office, and she would close the door? I told him you know why; he would smile.

Everyone would ask me what you and Pam are doing behind closed doors; I told them, she wants me to rub her shoulders, this was also going on before we went to Palm Springs from time to time. She was my supervisor and I had to do what she asked me to do, at least to a certain extent. She asked me to do a couple other things, but I refused to do everything she asked, the only reason I did what she asked was because of her illness. But after she bye pass me for the promotion, I made sure that I stopped going to her office; she would still call me to come into her office, but I made excuses, or I would just say I am busy, she finally started getting the message. There was no attraction on my part from the very beginning, all the attraction was on her part. Like I said earlier I had already done that older white woman shit! I was not going back there, at least not with Pam! We talked about our situation about a month later and I told her I was glad I never laid up with her; especially after the way she did me with the promotion. I told her she would have held that sexual act over my head for the remaining time I was under her supervision; I said that one day we were talking, I also told her the worst thing a man can do to a woman is turn her down especially when a woman is trying her best to give herself to him. Because men will take almost any and everything that will come his way, because men are vulnerable. I told her she tried her best to start a relationship with me; but I did not want it. I told her I am glad I turned her down, she started to tear up. I told her she might be prejudice, but her pussy is not! Men could say no to women just like a women can say no to a man. That is the reason she wanted me so bad I left her office after that comment; I was thinking what charges she going to bring toward me for what I said, is she going to try to fire me because I said her pussy was not prejudice that would have insinuated that she offered me the pussy, so she did not try to make a big deal out of my comment, she never wanted this conversation to come up again. We continued working together for about another year maybe two, but the relationship was not as good as it was prior, I was still cool and respectful to her, she would be looking out the corner of her eyes, the thought of me turning Pam down continue to bother her until her health started to suffer and she retired, I ended up leaving PST and working for one of the Sarah's that did not want to hire me prior to Pam's retirement. I am not a bad guy, I am not a mean guy, but how much shit can a man take? Carol ended up being my supervisor in the future of my employment, she could not look me in the eye after she received the assistant supervisor position because she knows she did not earn it, she was given the position. It is hard for a person to deal with someone that they knew deep down inside they did not beat out, you are going to find this out after you continue to read this story.

WHAT IS THIS NIGGER DOING WITH THIS NICE MERCEDES BENZ?

After being sabotage at So-low and sexually harassed; it was time for the next person to step up with their stupidity. This woman was the office manager at the time, she was a white woman, every one called her Willie. In or around the year of two thousand four my wife and I purchased a used two thousand three Mercedes Benz E320. I had always wanted a Benz; the color is Pewter. Pewter is like a silver or champagne color; it is a sweet ride and I still look good in it today. Pewter might even be my color; I think it goes with my eyes. As I write this with a smile on my face.

Back to Willie, co-workers would tell me to watch out for Willie, she would sometime choose a person to mess with, I did not pay too much attention to her I figure if she mess with me, then I will deal with it at that time, plus I never really dealt with her, we very seldom cross paths.

I remember one time my daughter was going on a field trip to a well- known campground in Northern California; I had never had a problem with Willie, I had a co-worker tell me Willie lived near this campground, I had never been to this campground and my wife, and I was feeling uncomfortable about our daughter going up there without someone we knew and trusted. She was going with the schools, but it still was not enough for us to feel comfortable with our daughter going up there alone, after all she is only about seven or eight years old at the time.

The schools had all the chaperones they needed; so, I could not get in at the last minutes, my wife told me I had to drive up to the campground so we will know exactly where it was located, so I took

51

off work and followed the school buses to the campgrounds. My daughter did not know I was following her bus; the campground was approximately two hours away. Once we reached the campgrounds; I spoke to one of the Camp Rangers, he assured me my child would be fine and she would have fun during her stay, she was going to be there for about three days and two nights, my daughter did not know I spoke to the Rangers. The Rangers told me not to worry they are on the grounds around the clock twenty-four-seven. My daughter had her cell phone with her, so I drove home and told my wife I would talk to Willie, our office manager and ask her if I can get her number and I can give her my number just in case an emergency happens, we can get someone up to the campgrounds to help her and the other children.

The next morning I went to Willie's office and I asked her if it is OK for us to exchange our numbers for this reason, Willie said she would be happy to help my daughter if we needed it I gave her my number and she gave me hers, I felt good she would do that for me, because she did not have to help me, Willie actually live about five miles away from the camp site. I told her thanks this is greatly appreciated; I said you do not know how much this mean to me, my daughter went camping had fun and returned home safely, I let Willie know and I thanked her again.

Then approximately three weeks later Willie was getting into William's truck; he was an older gentleman, and he was a good man, father, and grandfather, he had his daughter her husband and his grandson living with him and his wife. William and I was pretty good friends, he used to tell me that his grandson was racing mini go-carts around the state of California, William built his grandson a go-cart in his garage from the ground up, he made sure the go-cart had all the official specifications that the racing association stated they needed to qualify. Matter of fact I told William to let me know when his grandson would be racing around Fairfield, and I will come and watch him. His grandson was racing in Vallejo one Saturday morning; I got up and went and watched him compete in about three races, his grandson placed first in one race and had two second place finishes. I met William's wife, daughter, her husband, and his grandson that day.

Back to Willie and William, they were getting into William's truck I do not know where they were headed; that was first time I had ever seen them two riding together, about fifteen minutes prior to me seeing them leaving I went on my brake. This was also the first time I had drove my Mercedes Benz to work. I had my Benz for about two years and had never drove it to work. I parked my car across the street in this furniture store parking lot, I was not sure if I wanted my co-workers to see my car. My mother had told me sometimes you cannot always let people see what you got, sometime people would get jealous of what you have, so I parked the car across the street. I went on brake before William and Willie was leaving; I went to the Der Weiner Schnitzel to get me a breakfast burrito as I was driving back, I decided to park in So-Low's parking lot, I saw a parking spot right at the end of the lot near the entrance, I pulled into the parking spot real easy, why did I do that? Willie and William happen to be getting in Williams truck at the same time I was parking and was getting out of my car. I had on my black Ray Bans sun glasses so they could not see my eyes but I can see their eyes; Willie was just staring at me as I got out of my car, William was not pay any attention to me he was just driving out of the parking lot, but Willie had her eyes trained on me she was looking at me to the point it made me feel uncomfortable, I continued in to the building while they drove off. When I got into my office; the look I received was still bothering me, so I decided to put a notation on my desk calendar, Willie gave me derogatory look this Friday when I was entering the building, my supervisor Mrs. Hilton was not in the office that day because she took off work every payday Friday to hang out with her grandkids.

The following Monday morning when I got to work; Mrs. Hilton came in my office at about nine o'clock am, she asked me was I late for work last Friday? I told her no. Then she asked was I late from brake? I told her no I was not late from brake, I glanced at my desk calendar and asked Mrs. Hilton, why, what did Willie tell you? She stated Willie did not tell me anything, I told Mrs. Hilton yes she did! What did she say? Mrs. Hilton said, Willie said, I was either late for work or late from brake, I told her to tell Willie I was not late for work or brake, I told her to ask Willie do she know what time I left that past Friday morning, I knew she did not know when I left because as I told you before, I parked my car across the street, Willie office was upstairs and she had a walk way outside her window on the second floor, when I walked out of the building on the ground level after taking the elevator down, I walked out of the door, turned right immediately and walked up under the walk way outside of Willie's office, so there was no way she could have seen me leaving the building, she seen me returning only.

My questions made Willie get a hair up her ass toward me; so, she started to investigate me and my work, she decides to pull my phone records to try to get me for making personal calls, she went back two years in my phone records both incoming and outgoing calls to try to get me for personal calls. She took our Child Support Case Investigator off his Child Support Cases he was working and had him investigating me, he was calling all the 510 numbers because that was the area code I grew up in, she had him calling all the 707 numbers because that is the area code I lived in, she had him call all the 925 numbers, because that is the area code my wife worked in, I had my own cell phone at this time when I wanted to make a personal call. Like President Chump would say, she went on a witch hunt! I told all my Black friends if they wanted to ever curse out a white police officer now is the time! One time, I walked in the bathroom and Duane was at one of the urinals, I walked up next to him and said Duane what is happening? he responded by saying same O! Same O! I said you are still investigating me. He said no! He said he thought it was stupid ideal at the beginning; a couple of my friends and one of my sister's was called by him. One of my friends told me he curse him out! I felt bad for him because the friend he spoke to probably curse the shit out of him. Duane said in his opinion, I never had a personal call problem, I told Duane he did not find a problem because I did not have problem with personal calls. I said Duane; how can I have a problem with personal calls when I am one of the top collectors in the office; I spent most of my time collecting on my cases. Willie made up some personal calls which gave her reasons to suspend me for two weeks without pay anyways, it was all bullshit! She knew it and I knew it! So, I had to take two weeks off and did not receive a paycheck for those two weeks, when I returned to work. I called the administrative office prior to not receiving my paycheck; I spoke to the Administrative Manger her name Helen, I asked her if I can payback the two weeks in three or four-hundred-dollar increments, because I have a family to support, that way I can still receive a partial paycheck.

Helen responded to me by saying no way; it would not be a punishment if she did not take it all at once; this was a white woman who did not care about my family. I said I understand; you do not care about my kids and my family, before she said another word, I hung up on her ass and called her a bitch to myself, I was not going to beg her for anything. Her stupidity and lack of respect for her fellow county employees did not stop me from surviving, I was always taught to adapt and overcome, when you run into a person like Helen who cannot feel for others deep down in her soul, she is a lonely person, her soul is empty, she will spend the rest of her life with no real friends, because

55

she does not have a real heart, you get what you give to others, and if someone cannot feel for another person kids or family then deep down inside their own soul is empty and lonely, the only people that will love them is their family, their family will stop loving them also when they figure out that she is a cold hearted person, so her day is coming, a cold hearted person will always have their day. That goes for Willie also, for something insignificant as car would bother her to the point, she would want to ruin another employee's job shows she is an empty person, sole is none existing, and it tell you a lot about a person life.

They also decided to take my office away from me; they relocated me to a cubicle outside of my supervisor's office Mrs. Hilton, they did this all while my Hispanic co-worker was sleeping in his office daily. Bob use to always say they do not have time to mess with him, because they are too busy messing with the brother! He would laugh at me every time. Like I said I was always taught to adapt and overcome adversity; shit I did not have a day in my life I did not have any adversity, adversity is survival in most Black people's lives. The first day I was to sit in my cubicle; I walked into my cubicle outside of my supervisor's office. The other supervisor who did not want to hire me name Sarah left a cubicle etiquette paper in my seat; the paper was telling me what to eat in a cubicle, things I can eat in a cubicle without bother other people in my area. The Sarah who interviewed me and did not want to hire me, she has never been my supervisor, it puzzled me why someone will just fuck with another person and do not have justification or reasoning for doing such an act, I had not said ten words to this individual since my interview. Just one answer I can come up with; it starts with the letter B, she felt compel to leave this document in my chair, it proves hatred toward another person runs over weekends, she was obviously thinking of me over the weekend for her to take the time to come up with this crap. I was pissed off; I was thinking these motherfucker's do not have

56

anything else to do over the weekend; but find a way to fuck with me, yes hatred run over the weekend. It is a twenty four hour a day gig for some white folks; I was not thinking of them at all over my weekends; but they were obsessed with me for some reason, I knew what the reason was deep down inside, you can try to sugar coat the reason but as a person bite into chocolate you will eventually get to the cherry, in this case the cherry is the racist truth. So I walked around the office and asked people if they left this letter on my chair; I got to the other supervisor name Sarah, she was the other Sarah in my interview who did not want to hire me, I asked her did she leave this letter in my chair before she said yes, I seen it in her eyes, she was the person who left the letter. I just shocked my head and walked away in discuss; I walked down to our Director's Tim office, I asked him was he aware that Sarah put this document in my chair, he told me yes! I asked did he approve this action, he said yes, he approved it. I told him Thanks! Then I walked off and went back to my cubicle. They also took my incoming phone line away; any clients that want to contact me directly, could not! They would have to call the witch board operator and get transferred to me, they screened all my calls they wanted to know exactly who I was talking too, when, and why!

My supervisor at the time Mrs. Hilton; she stated she wanted me to turn in a document with all the account numbers I worked each day; she reviewed each account and sent all the accounts back to me to do somethings else to each account every day, she knew by having me work the same accounts again, it would put me behind in my work. That is exactly what it did; it would make my job that much harder to complete; they were basically trying to get me to quit, but that was not going to happen, it was not an option. I was not going to lose my pose and say something that was going to get me terminated, nothing was going to stop me from supporting my family. I was also the type of person that was taught winner never quit and quitters never win.

So, I decided to go on the offense; I start wondering what I can do to disrupt their days like they are disrupting my days. So, I started singing in my cubicle; you see my cubicle was right outside of Mrs. Hilton office, I was also about fifteen feet from the other supervisor named Sarah, they both can hear every word I said. So, I started singing old Negro spiritual songs; Like: Old happy days! We shell over come! Wade in the water! Swing Low Sweet Chariot! Amazing Grace! I mixed in a few Impressions songs like Keep on Pushing! James Brown, "Say it loud I am Black and I'm proud", I also threw in a bunch of Motown songs. I song all day, every day, whenever I hung up my phone I started singing. These songs were driving Mrs. Hilton crazy, she would ask me to quit singing, I told her singing was good for my soul; it was also good therapy it helped me deal with the stress that came along with the child support job. If they were going to fuck with me; I was going to fuck with them, I thought I sound good if I said so myself.

They kept me in the cubicle approximately two or three years, before they gave me back my office; co-workers use to come by my cubicle to look in it like I was exhibit at the zoo. I just kept on singing my Negro spirituals, George Benson "Masquerade"; Temptation's; Maze; Whispers and making sure it was driving any and everyone around me crazy. I enjoyed every minute of it; because I knew it was driving them insane. As soon as I enter my cubicle, I would start sing each morning and all day, I knew I was beating the shit out of them without laying a hand on them, I song those songs every day for two or three years straight, I made sure I drove them nuts. That is called good trouble!

Mrs. Hilton eventually could not take my singing any longer and gave me back my office after about three years; she also got tired of sending my work back to me after all by me turning my work into Mrs.

Hilton was giving her extra work to do also, so she told me I did not have to turn in my work every day any longer. Child Support is a job where each employee made their own decision on how they wanted to handle their cases; my decision may not be the same as your decision each case was handle differently by everyone, each employee made their own call on their cases just because I handled my case a certain way, did not mean you had to handle your case the same way.

Mrs. Hilton was basically giving me her own opinion on the way she would work my cases; I did not agree with her decision, so I never really made the changes she wanted me to make, plus making all her correction would have been too time consuming, I just continued to working the cases the way I choice too, my way was better anyways because each month I was one, two or three in collections each and every month in our division. Plus, I had already made an agreement with the non-custodial or custodial parent on the case; I was not going to go back on my word and change the agreement after we came to an amicable agreement. Some time she would get petty and nick-pick on her responses; like one time she asked me to call the custodial parent and ask her how much she weighted, because we did not have the custodial parent weight on our computer system and in most cases the custodial is a woman, she wanted me to call the custodial parent not to talk about her money, but she wanted me to ask the mother how much she weighted, I told her she is crazy if she think I was going to do that, "I said that to myself". I just did not do it. I continue to work my cases.

They gave me back my office; but not my phone line they gave my old phone extension to a new employee who came in, I was the only employee who did not have his own outside extension line. My clients use to ask me all the time why they cannot call me directly; I told them the truth because if management was going to continue to disrespect me, I was not going to try to cover their bullshit! If they did not care, then I did not care either.

Mrs. Hilton was a woman who talked about her ex-husband a lot; she talked about how no good he was, she would say she gave her life up for the man and he left her for a younger woman, she said he was a real dog! I think she had a soft spot for me deep inside; when I told her that I was writing a book of poetry, she bought me three Maya Angelo's books, I greatly appreciated, but when she started running with Willie bullshit; let just say, I did not appreciate her as much. Willie had a son that was about my age or a little younger; he started showing up at the job and picking Willie up, she must have told him around the time I took my afternoon break, because he would be outside in the parking lot. I started parking my car across the street from the job again, when all this bullshit started, I did not park my car on the county parking lot for approximately ten years after the incident. I boycotted the county parking lot; I had one other co-worker name Lisa a Hispanic woman she was living with another women she felt they had mistreated me, so she decided not to park in the county lot. Lisa was from So Cal in one of the Hispanic Urban areas down south. Willie's son would cut his eyes at me some time he would be in his monster truck; one of those trucks that sit high off the ground, one day I looked at him and I asked him if he had a problem? He said no; I went across the street and started dribbling my basketball I kept in the back of my car and listen to some music, he did not want anything to do with me at least not man to man maybe if he had a few friends with him, then he would have found some heart, I am sure he came up to see me because he had never came up there before or at least I had never seen him before.

I also contacted the state agency, I had to use the Sacramento Office of DFEH, who I soon found out they are as useless as So-Low. It is not that DFEH is a terrible organization; it is just the office near

60

my office was a terrible office to file a complaint. You will find out exactly what I am talking about as you continue to read on. During the first year of being place in a cubicle; I decided I was not going to start taking this shit so I decide to file a formal complaint against So-Low CSD for unfair treatment and working in a hostile environment. By me being a Black man, they did not think I knew my employment rights; I filed the complaint with the nearest office. I had to use the Sac office because that was the closest office to my place of employment; I went to my intake interview, my case was reviewed by a Black woman, she listen and took notes for about an hour and a half, I submitted all the necessary documents, dates and times, everything the department needed to determine if I had a legitimate case, she told me I was definitely unfairly treated and she will forward documents to the investigators to investigate my complaint, she said one of the investigators will contact me within a week.

I received a call a few days later; it was a Mexican woman, we talked over the phone for about twenty minutes, she agreed to investigate my complaint, she sent the investigation documents to So-Low for them to complete. I told her to be prepared for So-Low to lie; when So-Low realized I had file a complaint against them with the state agency, that is when I started receiving looks out of the side of their heads, they would be walking by me and would not say hi or get quit, I did not care how they felt, they did not care how I felt. They investigate the complaint and after So-Low fed them all their lies and bullshit they could not continue my investigation; I asked representative to give me a copy of So-Low's response to my complaint; I read over their response to my complaint and I was right, they lied! I debated their responses, I asked state representative to setup a mediation between So-Low and myself, she decided to side with So-Low, and issued me a right to sue letter. Which give me that right to get an attorney to help me within a year if

I decided to go that route. If you remember I took a large pay cut when I accepted the job at So-Low so it was no way I can continue to raise my family and paying an attorney; I had one year to get an attorney. I pursued a few Attorney's; their fees was much more then I could afford at that time, or wanted to afford, one attorney in San Francisco wanted ten thousand down to take my case, he was a Black man and he wanted ten grand down, I laughed; I thought he was joking when he told me his retainer fee amount, I was happy for him but I was not going to give him ten thousand, even if I had it; which I did not! I thought he could help me; but what if he was not able to help me, he was a high powered attorney because his office was located on the fifteen floor, right downtown San Francisco on Market St. which is the high rent district of the city, I asked him to consider taking my case on a pro-bono basis but he refused, he stated it was too far to travel it would have been at least a two hour drive for him from the city.

I thought about quitting and looking for another job, but remember what I said earlier "winners never quit and quitters never win" plus I am married to a Black woman; have you ever lived with a Black woman and had no job? It was not worth the agony, tongue lashing and ass whooping's that will go along with the unemployment status and I could not put my family in that situation.

So, I figured maybe these knuckleheads would leave me alone. Since they realized I knew the proper avenues to sue their asses. I continue to work there and set back to see what they were going to come up with next. They stayed away from me for about a year. Lucky me!

LESTER

Lester is someone I will never forget; one day Lester walked into our office and asked for assistance with his child support case, he had just been released from Pelican Bay State Prison in Northern California which is one of the worse prisons in the country. This is the worse prison in the state of California they housed the most hardened criminals in Pelican Bay State Prison that are not sentence to death. Some of the worse gang members from every gang is being housed at this facility; Pelican Bay State Prison is the only Super Max Prison located in the state of California. They called Carol to assistant him; she was the friend I use to have lunch with she always wanted to prove how tough she was, she told Lester she cannot release his license without at least a thousand dollars down he left the office very angry that day.

Approximately a week later he came back into the office; he was very upset at our office, Carol was out to lunch when he came in, our PST receptionist called me when she realized he was fresh out of prison. I walked out of my office and walked up to booth with bullet proof glass separating us and called Lester's name, I started to sit down, and I glanced up and saw one of the biggest Mexican I have ever seen walking up to the booth, I thought he was going to rip the bullet proof glass out of the wall. This man was about six feet two, weighted about two hundred and thirty-five pounces, he was cut tight, thin waist, had some big ass arms, when he set down, he was blocking all the sun light behind him outside. I said what can I do for you? He was upset, he said I came in here last week and I got some lady who told him she cannot get his license back without a thousand dollars down. He said Sir, I just got out prison two weeks ago, he said I am Mexican, my mother does not have a

63

thousand dollars to give him for child support or anything else, he said my dad died years ago, he said the only way for him to get a thousand dollars down is to violate my parole. I said we do not want that; I told him he is no good to me and his child locked up, he said he has been incarcerated since he was twelve years old, he had been incarcerated off and on for the majority of his young life, he had the scares to prove the hard time he had completed, he stated he was in juvenile hall on three separate occasion between the age of twelve and eighteen because of gang activity, drug possession and selling drugs. The third time he was incarcerated it was because of arm robbery; this carries a mandatory sentence of ten to fifteen years. He was about thirty-six at the time we was talking but he was sixteen when he caught the armed robbery case, he spend two years in juvenile and then he had to go to the penitentiary, he served time in all the California prison Susanville, San Quentin, Mule Creek State Prison, Salinas all of them, he had even serve time in the state of Oklahoma at the state prison nicknamed "Big Mac", sometimes because of over crowdedness they will ship an inmate to another state to serve out their time, he just got released from Pelican Bay State Prison where he spent the last four years of his life, he violated his parole and received a four year sentence in Pelican Bay; he spent two year of the sentence on the famous Pelican Bay Shu which means you are housed with the most harden criminals in the state of California, he was locked down twenty three hours a day, you get a hour shower one day, the next day he get hour in an eight by eight walled in area, you can only see the sky, he said he was glad to be out of there. He also stated within the last four years of his sentence he studies and received his high school diploma; he also earned his electrician's certification. He had only seen his daughter one time since he was incarcerated last time, his daughter was not one years old the last time he saw her, he saw her for the first time a couple days prior, he said his daughter is staying with the grandmother on the mother side because her mother is in a rehabilitation center for meth use, meth was huge in So-Low along with OxyContin, she had approximately six months to complete in a twenty-four hour rehabilitation center. I told him I was going to help him out; I told him I was going to give him his driver license back, he asked how much I wanted down, I told him I do not want anything down; he said what are you talking about nothing down? That is when Carol retuned from lunch and she walk past the booth, he saw her, he said that is the woman who wanted a thousand down, I told him I knew who he was talking about, because Carol always wanted to show how tough she was, I knew it was her. I told him do not worry about it, I said how long will it take him to locate work? He told me he will have a job in sixty days; I told him I am going to release his license for ninety days. I told him if he does not have a job in ninety days, to call me and I will be extended the license release if needed. I asked him was he clean because he will have to pass a drug test, he said yes, he is clean, and he must stay clean while he is on parole. He said he is randomly drug tested; he cannot take that chance, he said he is tired of being incarcerated, so he will not do anything to jeopardize his freedom and seeing his daughter grow up. I released his license; he was grateful and happy that I helped him out. I told him just keep his word with me; I said do what you say you are going to do, and we will never have a problem. I used to say, you take care of me, and I will take care of you, he left the office and went to DMV to get his license.

Two months later he walks in our office with his new job information; he also had his daughter with him; he said he brought his daughter so she can meet the man who showed some faith in him and was willing to believe in him. He told me the gang he was with while incarcerated was all Hispanic; he said he did not think I was going to help him, I told him he is not locked up any longer, now that he is out he does not know who might help him, he gave me all his employment paperwork so I can issue a wage and medical assignment, he will have medical coverage for his child in thirty days. He was holding his daughter in the booth and I was telling him how pretty she is; while I was looking at her, I asked him if she has chickenpox's, he said no, he said his daughter live with her grandmother and her grandmother had four cats and three dogs running around the house, he said his daughter is on the floor with the animals and her grandmother does not keep the house clean. I looked at the little girl through the bullet proof glass; she must have had two hundred flea bites all over her body, on her legs, torso, arms, back and face. I asked Lester what is his living situation? He stated he lives with his mother and her boyfriend, I asked him how many bedrooms the house, he said three, he said his mother and boyfriend is in one room, he is in another room, I said your daughter could have the other room, he said yeah, she could have the other room. He said his mother would love to have her granddaughter living there; I said do you have any animal, he said his mother has a little lap dog, I asked him if his mother or her boyfriend ever had any problems with the law, he said no. I asked him if his mother would be willing to take his daughter; he said yes, she would be willing to take his daughter, he said his mother was upset last night because she never get to see her granddaughter. I asked him if he can get his mother to come into our office so I can meet her. He said what are you trying to do? I told him I am trying to get his daughter under his mother's care, because his daughter cannot continue to live in her current environment. I told him by law I must report incident like this; I cannot give the child to him because he is felon, she can live in the same home with him, but the legal custody must go to his mother. I asked him was his mother working, he said they are both retired. I told him to take his daughter over to Child Protected Service; I called one of my contacts over at CPS, told her the situation, she said have

66

him bring the child to their office so they can have a medical doctor examine her. I told Lester to take his little girl over to CPS right now and ask for Sue; I told him where CPS was located, I also told him to contact his mother and let her know there is a chance she may receive temporary guardianship of your child, let her know she need to clean up the house if needed, because CPS may come by today, he said my mother's home is always clean, I said good answer, I told him to call his mother as he walked down to CPS let her know we are reviewing his case again, she may receive temporary guardianship for now, them it could turn into permanent guardianship in the future, that's if her mother does not clean up her act after her rehabilitation stay and after she go through the step within the court system. I told him we have to get your baby out of that household now, she cannot be on the floor with all those dogs, cats and fleas at the grandmother house, she cannot stay in this unsafe environment.

He took his daughter to CPS and met with Sue; Sue took all the necessary steps to change guardianship after she had chance to review the child, take pictures and have a medical doctor examine her. Once Lester's mother got the news that it was a possibility that she can get custody of her granddaughter; she jumped at the opportunity of getting guardianship, she drove from Sacramento to So-low which was about forty five minutes away, she met with Sue, she told her the process she was going to have to complete in order to get the child in her custody; Sue went to Lester's mother home that same evening and left the baby with them that night, Sue also contact the grandmother on the mother's side of the family and told her CPS was going to change the custody order because of the physical condition of the child and because of the child's environmental living conditions are unsafe. The grandmother on the mother's side did not put up much of a fight; I believe she was happy to get rid of her granddaughter, it was hard for me to understand how she can release her granddaughter so easily, she was a beautiful little girl, plus So-Low was looking at the possibility of charging the grandmother with child neglect. Lester's mother was glad to have her; Lester's mother got up the next morning, she and her granddaughter drove to my office because she had to meet the man who helped her get custody of her granddaughter. She was so happy and thankful; she started crying in the booth; she just kept saying thank you. I almost started to tear up myself, I walked around to the lobby on the other side of the bullet proof glass; I put my arms around her and I told her I was glad I can help her and her granddaughter, his mother was an older Hispanic lady, looked like she was in her mid to late sixties, she was telling me thank you for putting a smile on her son face. She said he just made one bad turn after another while he was young; she had not seen him smile like this since he was a child. All this took place in or around mid-May; I believe he was release from prison in March, he got to see his daughter for the second time in both of their lives in March, he got his job by mid-May his daughter was living with him by the beginning of June. I was happy I was able to help his daughter; by getting her a better living situation and help her dad and grandmother out. I really felt good about myself; I continued doing my job to the best of my ability.

In or around the end of July Lester's mother came into my office with the little girl; she asked the receptionist to call me because she need to talk to me about something, I came out and met her in one of the booths up front, she and her granddaughter set down, his mother and I looked at each other and she just started crying. I gave her a Kleenex tissue she dried her eyes, then she told me Lester died! I said no he did not! She said he passed away on July the fourth; she said he got to enjoy his daughter's company for about thirty days. She said Harry, he loved you for what you did to help him and his daughter. He was so thankful, his mother said he would talk about you on a daily base and how happy he was to get me when he walked in our office. We both started crying at this time I could not believe he passed away, she stated he had a massive heart attack on the fourth of July and fell out in the house; they called the ambulance and when they arrive he was in bad shape, she said he passed on the way to the hospital, she said he told her while he was incarcerated he was taught not to trust Blacks, Whites and Asians. She said you changed his entire way of thinking by what you did; his mother told me I was a real bright spot in his life, she hugs me again and told me thanks you for making her son smile before he passed away. This incident still is embedded in my heart; it will stick with me for the remainder of my life. I told his mother if she ever needs me for anything do not hesitate to contact me concerning her granddaughter. I spoke to Lester's mother a couple more times concerning the possible benefits that his daughter could receive; after that conversation I never heard from her again. I just prayed that his daughter grows up and become a nice adult, I believe his daughter would be almost twenty years old now. Rest in peace Lester!

JACKIE

This incident was something I was totally surprised to find myself in especially since I have always had nothing but the upmost respect for handicap individuals; I have always tried to be as courteous and thoughtful to handicap people, I never parked in their parking spot, I told my kids I better not catch or hear them teasing kids who are less fortunate or anyone with a mental or physical disability. A lady who worked in our office, I believe her right side has been disable due to a car accident, she's been working there for about fifteen years before I started my employment.

She was nice to me, she even invited me to a couple of her parties she threw; I attended two of her parties and had a nice time while I was there. The parties started after work; I would go to the parties and leave by about eight o'clock at night, she would have a keg and some hard liquor also, some of the employee's would be smoking weed, she had some good weed, this was before weed was legalized in the states. She also reminded me of a flower child; she was kind of a free spirit, I thought she was cool. I had worked with her for about seven or eight years at this time, I liked her as a person, we had always had a good rapport that is why this next incident surprised the shit out of me.

One day I was leaving for lunch; I took the elevator down to the ground level and was exiting the building, I open the door, I saw her walking up to the door she was about ten feet from the door, so I held the door for her as she approached the door, I said what I always said to her and other coworkers "what happening young lady?" "How are you doing"? She looked at me and cut her eyes at me, she said Harry why do you always have to ask me how I'm I doing? I said I did not mean anything negative, so I let the door close and went to lunch when I returned from lunch, I got called in to my supervisor office, my supervisor at this time was cubicle etiquette the other supervisor who did not want me in my first interview. We had a reorganization and I land under her supervision; we are going to call her cubicle etiquette from this point on.

When I entered cubicle etiquette's office, she said she received a complaint from Jackie stating she did not want me to ask her how she is doing any longer. I said what is wrong with me asking someone how they are doing. She said Jackie is sometime moody, she asked me to have you stay away from her. I worked on the opposite side of the building on the second floor from her office. I asked cubicle etiquette, what if I must use the fax machine; it was on Jackie's side of the building, matter of fact it was right outside of her office. Cubicle etiquette told me to stay away from that side of the building; if I need to fax a document, she said I need to ask a co-worker to fax the documents for me.

I walked away from her office thinking these motherfuckers are stupid! These motherfuckers cannot be this stupid; I thought I was in an episode of the Twilight Zone! "I said all this to myself". My punishment was I could not walk down to the other side of the building, some of my co-worker told me if I needed to fax any documents, they would fax them for me. After about thirty days of this shit. I decided to report this incident to my union and to the state agency again.

Because I do not like people fucking with me unnecessarily, I told them I walk out of the building to go to lunch. By the time I return to work I am band from one side of the entire building in about thirty minutes; because I said "what's happening" to my co-worker and held the door open for her. I reported it to my union they did absolutely nothing; I told our state agency office in Sacramento about the band in the office, they did absolutely nothing, I believe they got scared because she had a disability. "I guess Disabilities Trumps Racism", I did not have anything against her disability I treated her like I believe all people desire to be treated, with "Respect"! That goes for disabled people or not. I believe if everyone respected each other we would not have all the crap in the world today.

Respect is free! It is one thing I learned while working in So-Low CSD is you never know what other people has gone through in their lives. Everyone has a different story that is why I tried my best to treat everyone I assisted with respect. Plus, you never knew who you are dealing with. They might come back and shoot you in your ass. You think I am playing? Within the last ten years of my employment, I knew at least four or five men who committed suicide over their child support. That's why I said, you do not know who you are dealing with or their situation.

One of the gentlemen called the custodial parent his ex-wife and told his children goodbye. He also called me and thank me for trying to him get his case current, I was letting him pay what he could afford, because I could not release his license without a payment. He could not get a job without a valid driver license. He kept running into what he called bad luck with his problems at home, his drinking, drug use and depression he was basically homeless. What little money he was able to earn he would come in and pay five dollars on his case. He told me he did not know what was going to happen to him. I told him not to do anything crazy; I knew he was unstable mentally, but it is tough to make a call on another adult stating he is unstable, so I did not call, I told him I would help him locate a job. He told me bye, Harry. He hung up, I never heard from him again. The Custodial parent called me the following week and told me he committed suicide by hanging. He hung himself at his parent's home in his bedroom. Unfortunately, I have a lot of stories like his.

Back to Jackie, I filed a complaint with my union and stay agency in the Sacramento Office and they did absolutely nothing; when So-Low heard I had filed another complaint they lift the band, but I was still in the cubicle. I was able to fax my own documents again after about three to four months of not walking on that side of the building, everyone on the other side of the building was welcoming me back to their side, they were also talking about how stupid of a rule they made for me. They told me Jackie had gotten mad at everyone in the building at one time or another. She ended up retiring a few years later, she was bitter toward the CSD, she would cut her eyes at me; she never said another word to me from that point on. Until this day, I still do not know why she dislike me so much before she retired. I guess it's because I asked people: "How they are doing"? Let's move on to the next crap!

FOUR SUPERVISOR POSITIONS

About a year after all the above crap. The So-Low CSD had four supervisor positions come available; we had a couple new hires who had been working there for about year or two. One young lady was a nice looking young white lady in her mid to late thirties; her office was near my cubicle, I was older than she and she enjoyed talking to me, she valued my advice because she was going through a divorce, and I made her laugh and got her mine off her problems.

She loved her husband, until he fucked up! She caught her husband laying up with another woman, she left him and took his dog with her, she stated he keep asking for his dog back, I always cracked up and thought it was funny. She said, she is going to keep his dog and he can keep the dog he was laying up with. I told her a dog is a man's best friend; she would say not anymore, she said he has his dog already, she said he can walk her for now on. I asked her if she was going to take his dog up in the hills and drive off, she said I cannot do that to the dog, she said, she would drive her ex-husband in the hills and let his ass go with no problem. I told her all men are vulnerable. She said no, all men are stupid! We cracked up! We always had fun while working together. I like her because she was feisty and funny. She liked my collection style; I told her you cannot talk to people like you was a straight lace white boy, I told her a straight lace white person is the last person people want to talk too especially when they are having financial problems. I told her when you get the person on the phone you have to talk to them and get a feel for what type of person you are dealing with; once you get a feel for the person, you are talking to then talk to them in a language or slang they understand, she would hear me in my cubicle, and I would be talking all kinds of shit to my client. Like if you do not pay your support the Federal Government, State Government, and every other government will bend them over and break them down, like they have never been broken down before. I would start sing the song, "Child Support will make you hurt so bad, "it make you hurt so bad"! I would tell them this will never go away it is going to haunt you the rest of your life if you do not take care of it.

One day we were sitting around at work; I asked her is she going to interview for one of the vacant supervisor positions, she said she did not know; I told her she should go for it, I told her she was perfect for the position, she said what do you mean by that? I told her she fit the profile perfectly for the position; I told her she is blond hair and blue eyed, she said that is the reason why I will get the position, I told her around here it will help her. So, we place a little side bet; she was qualified for position, but she had only been there for a very short period less than two years, we bet twenty dollars. She completed an application. She ask was I going to complete an application. I told her no I been there and done that, I told her good luck! Her main competition was a bunch of Mexican women with more years of experience.

The Mexican co-workers had years of experience in the division ranging from five years to twenty or thirty years of experience; but that still was not enough in this racist office. One Mexican lady had over twenty years; she had tried for a supervisor position on more than one occasion, she was turned down on more than one occasion also, management kept telling her to take all these supervisor classes offered through So-Low, she took and passed every class, they still turned her down. She was very knowledgeable, I always asked her questions or for her opinion on cases; she was a nice Mexican lady who was willing to help anyone who needed help, she had some personal tragedies in her life, she just leaned on the Lord make it through and found comfort. There were other Mexican representatives who qualified for the positions; there was about six co-workers I can think off the top of my head, they all interviewed for the supervisor positions there was another young white woman representative, one day I walked pass her office, she was filling out a document on her computer, I creeped up behind her, I said girl what are you doing? I scared her because her back was too me. She said I am filling out an application for the assistance supervisor position, I told her while she is at it, fill out an application for one of the supervisor positions, I told her all they can say is no! She completed an application for one of the supervisor positions. She also fit the profile perfectly.

Management completed their interviewing process for the four supervisor positions; they announced the position over the loudspeaker and four blond haired blue eyes received the positions. Even the assistance supervisor position was filed by a blond hair blue eyed woman. All the Mexican women was overlooked and by passed for the positions; I felt bad for them, they was mad and heartbroken and I could not blame them. Anna walked over and gave me my twenty dollars. Teri got one of the supervisor positions instead of the assistance supervisor position she initially applied for. I told Anna; I told you so, she just shook her head, I cracked up even though it was not funny. She soon moved downstairs and started her new supervisor position; I told her she was smart enough to handle the position, I told her I was proud of her, she ended up getting tired of the demands of the supervisor position. She soon realized she did not want to be a supervisor not because she could not handle the job; she did not like the other supervisors she was working with, she ended up moving out of the state about a year later. She moved somewhere in the Mideast area of the USA; I would see her ex-husband driving around town after she moved away, he was a delivery driver and yes, she took his dog with her. Next crap!

SPANISH SPEAKER PLEASE!

At the CSD in So-Low we had thousands of Mexican custodial and non-custodial parents come into our office. We also had a lot of Mexican's working in the office; not all of them spoke Spanish, some Mexicans did not like the other Mexicans because they did not speak Spanish.

One of my male Mexican co-worker who grew up in the states and did not speak Spanish; he said Mexican women from Mexico was no good and cannot be trusted. I used to say what you are talking about Willis. He said they cannot be trusted; he also said they have fucked up attitudes, they believe they are better than Mexican women and man from the states, rather they can speak Spanish or not, he would never go out with any women from Mexico.

Whenever a Mexican custodial or non-custodial parent called or walked in to get assistance with their case; we were told by the supervisors to get one of our Spanish speaking CS Assistance to translate our conversations for the non-Spanish speaking officers, this was a regular routine for the office. We had a pool of Spanish speaking CS assistance working in cubicles sitting together, there was only about five officers that spoke Spanish fluently. Whenever the officers need a Spanish speaker, everyone would walk over to their section and ask can someone speak and translate Spanish for us.

We had a Mexican woman working there with a green card to allow her to work and stay in the states; she seen to be a nice person, she had worked in our office for about one maybe two years. She enjoyed running in the endurance races, where you would be running, swim, and ride a bike for a certain number of miles, she had competed in a few races over the time I got to know her, she had a seven-year-old daughter who she started picking up and brought her into the office for her last two hours of work each day. After her daughter got comfortable around the office she would wonder away from her mother's cubicle; one day she had wonder far enough to reach my office; they gave me back my office by this time; this day the cute little Mexican girl stuck her head in my office, I looked up and said hi beautiful, she smiles and said hi. I asked the little girl what is your name? She said Lola. I said who is your mother? She said Maria. Maria walked over to my office told her daughter to stop bothering me, I told her she is not bothering me, I am enjoying the conversation, I gave her some candy I kept on my desk, and she left with her mother. After about two weeks of coming in my office every day Lola got to the point, she could not wait to get to the office to hang out with Uncle Harry. Maria told me her daughter love her some Uncle Harry; I would buy her something from the snack bar or a soda each day, we would talk while I was working my cases, sometimes I had to send her out of my office depending on who and what I was talking about, she would just wait outside until I was done then she would come back in and sit down.

Maria came into my office one day and we were just talking about what ever came to mind; she started talking about how tough it was to survive on her income, she was a single parent. I do not think she knew where Lola's dad was living, I believe he was back in Mexico somewhere. I don't ever remember Lola ever talking to me about her father; I could relate to Maria because I was making more money than she was, and my money was tight. I told her she just got to keep hanging, I told her my wife was getting rid of a lot of my daughter's clothes; I said the clothes is in good shape, they are all from Macy's or Nordstrom's, I told her I will bring them in and she can look through it and maybe she can find clothes that can fit Lola, she took all the clothes I brought her, I was glad to give them to her because I felt she really needed them and she appreciated my jester, I also loaned her twenty or forty dollars from time to time. She needed to get Lola some school supplies one time, I told her I will buy her a backpack. I asked Lola what her favorite color is; she said pink, I asked her if she like Barbie and she said yes! That weekend I asked my wife to pick up an extra backpack while she was at Target; I told her I was going to give it to Lola my little friend at work. I gave the backpack to Lola, she was so happy to receive it, it felt good to put a smile on the little girl's face. They even gave me one of her school pictures that I put on my refrigerator at home.

One day about a month later I was talking to Maria; she told me she does not like when the officers walk over to her section and ask can anyone speak Spanish for them. This method has been going on well before Maria had started working in the office; no one has ever complained about the method, she wanted the officers to go around to each assistant and ask them individually can they translate for them. By asking each person individually you might end up having to ask five different people, by asking everyone at one time you can get a volunteer who will come down to assist you. After all, this is their first language in many cases, I took her opinion with a grain of salt, this method had been working fine for years and the supervisors want you to start the case discussion with the client a.s.a.p., also all Spanish speakers are receiving extra pay for translating. I did not agree with her opinion and complaining to me did not amount to shit!

A couple weeks later; I received a call from the front desk stating I have a Spanish speaking walk in, I needed to go downstairs and meet with a Spanish speaking client. I got all my case work for this client together; I walked over to the translating section, I forgot about our conversations a couple weeks ago, I said I have a Spanish speaking client downstairs I need a Spanish speaker to translate for me please. I did not yell it; I asked loud enough that every one of the assistances could hear me. Maria jumped up and ran out of her cubicle; she came charging at me like a bat out of hell and said Harry! I told you not to come over to our section and ask for a Spanish speaker like that!!!! She said we do not come over to you and ask you how to cook Fried Chicken!!! Said it loud! Approximately ten co-workers heard her say it; I looked at her and said what does that have to do with needing a Spanish translator? I told her you have gone crazy! She stated, I told you not to do that, I told her I do not care about what to you told me. Another assistant said she would help me. Maria knew she had fucked up with me; some of my co-worker who heard her, told her you should not have said that to Harry, he did not deserve that! About three other co-workers and a supervisor reported her to our new director, a white woman at the time. Rhonda the director was pretty upset with the incident.

When I return from taking care of my client; I wanted to slap the shit out of that bitch, I went into my office and close the door. Man, women, and children all stayed away from me, a couple of older co-workers who had been working with me for years decided to check on me to make sure I was alright. I told them, yeah, I am fine. Some time I feel like I am surrounded by stupidity in this office.

Maria stopped her daughter from coming to my office; I heard she told our co-workers I tried to get her fired and she cannot talk to me any longer. She stated I tried to get her fired when in fact, I saved her job because four of my co-workers reported her to the new director. I told the new director in the meeting I did not want her terminated; she has her daughter she is taking care of; I did not want her daughter to suffer because of her mother's stupidity. Rhonda did not let her go, she did write her up; she was going to fire her, if I would have agreed to let her go. She stayed away from me, and she would not let her daughter come by my office any longer. Even though she would sneak by any ways to see Uncle Harry. Maria felt the tension in the air around the office and decided to start looking for another job. Ron my Mexican co-worker said Harry I told you them bitches are no good; I told him you sure did! I do not like calling women out of their names, but this bitch was crazier than a motherfucker.

It hurt me a little bit that I could not see my little friend every day. I was seeing her every day long enough to miss her; when she was no longer allowed to see me, talk to me, or look at me I told Maria to make sure she pays me my money back before she leaves, she paid me on our next payday, she left it on my desk, while I was helping another Spanish speaker downstairs. I did not change my method of asking for translator nor did I tell anybody my recipe for how to fry chicken.

A person must be crazy to have a green card in another country and willing to do something that could easily get her thrown out of the country. All it takes is for one of the higher position white representatives in the District Attorney's office to file a complaint and (ICE) Immigration and Customs Enforcement would walk her ass straight to the border; the District Attorney's Office is on first name bases with (ICE), I dealt with them myself on many occasions on cases over my twenty years of service. They would throw her little daughter out alone with her if she was not able to find someone to take care of her, even though she is a US citizen. President Chump would not have a problem separating them or just throwing them out together. She was lucky I did not press the issue or one of my white co-workers did not press the issue; I gave her a reprieve and she did not even know it. When she left, she still thought I tried to get her fired, she did not even realize I was one of her best friends in the office, even after all the things I done for her and her daughter. She was like a pit bulldog! Might bite the hands who feeds it. She bit the hand of a friend; it was her loss, I would run into her occasionally, at my gym, I had heard she moved to the same town I lived in, she would not say anything to me at the gym. Not even hi! That was fine with me, I did not want anyone with her attitude around me anyway, I was glad that Spanish speaking bitch was gone. Next crap!

FUNNY MONEY

One time during my employment there was some funny money being passed around town; it was starting to reach a lot of new restaurant and small businesses in the town; the town was expanding a little, new fast-food business started coming like Burger King, Carl's Jr's, Rally's Supermarket, even a Walmart was built across the street from our office. I would go to these different establishments and when I would receive my change back, I started receiving all these bills with derogatory statement written on both sides of the bills.

The bills were being defaced with red and black writing on the front and the back side of the bills; the different statements written on the bills, statements like "I hate the USA", "the USA is a bunch of crooks," "I hate the US Government". I would go get my lunch and received one of these bills back; I started receiving these bills frequently, I was thinking whoever is passing out those bills is going to be in a lot of trouble, when they get caught. We had another brother working with me for a short period time; he was an older gentleman who only needed about year to retire, I believe he transferred from another division because he was hurt on the job. He was cool; except for the time I called him brother, he told me we are not brothers, I turned and looked at him and said OK, "I am cool with that"! We did not let that come between us; I just did not call him my brother any longer. I did not put it together; the bills started coming around about the same time he starts working in our division, the bills were floating around local restaurants. He was giving his own case load to handle; he was quiet and stated in his office for the most part. He was a brother that did not relate well with other African American; he was like a prisoner who gave you the impression, he just wanted to do his time and get out. I kept my distance from him since he wanted it that way, we were friends, but we did not go to lunch together. He was what I call a five a day week friend, I respected him and he respected me.

One day I was coming back from lunch; I happened to be walking pass his office, I saw him hunched over like he was hiding something, the way his desk was position he could not see me walking up behind him, his back was to me, I walked up on him and said hey man what you doing? I surprised him when I walked up behind him, it was funny. He had a red and black marker sitting on his desk, he also had a stack of one-dollar bills on his desk, when I saw the markers and the stack of dollar bills on his desk, it all dawn on me that he was the one defacing the currency.

I said man; you are the person defacing US currency around here? I told him I been receiving these dollars with I hate the US Government written on them; I said do you know these white people would hang your ass for defacing US currency, I said you are defacing US currency while working in a US Government job, he was working for basically for the State of California which is a Government job, I told him this is a federal offense, I told him he would be looking at prison time, I said you know So-low would prosecute your ass for sure.

He said to hell with the US Government; he said they don't give a dam about us; he was listening to all these info-wars video against the US Government he gave me some videos to take home to watch. The videos were talking about how the US Government plan to take over the world and form a new world order. I told him after I seen the videos everybody knew something was going in the Government; I told him whenever you get a bunch of politicians together, you have a bunch of crocket individuals in one room, you have a room full of devils. Devils who believe they are superior to others; politicians are lawyers and what are lawyers called? Sharks! What do sharks do? Feed on the weak. You only hear from them when they need your vote. The other two or four years you will not hear from them other than on the TV; when you see them on TV, they are usually supporting something you are not supporting, they are pushing initiatives you do not agree with, most of the time they are pushing for what is best for them, not what is best for the country. You will also see them on TV when they are being prosecuted.

My brother who is not my brother was very angry at the US Government; I asked him if he voted, he said not anymore, he told me his vote do not mean shit, so he does not vote any longer. That somewhat angered me, I told him he should vote because at one time African Americans could not vote at all, I said thousands of African American died to give him the right to vote, I said the least he can do is get up and walk a couple of blocks to cast a ballot. He told me he is not casting shit; he said fuck casting a ballot. I said OK my brother! We started chuckling; I said Well go back to defacing his currency, I told him that is one way of making social change in the country, I do not know if it is the right way, this is your way to make progress for our race in our country, he yes. He asked was I going to tell on him; I told him no, I told him the only thing that will do is put another black man in prison, I said don't get caught, again! He went back to defacing of US currency. I went back to my office.

I had moved back into my office at this time. I thought to myself, Bob sleeping in his office and this knucklehead is defacing US currency right there in the building under their noses and they were fucking and suspending me because I owned a Mercedes Benz. How fucking dumb can these assholes around here be, and they call themselves managers.

There have been many of times I thought I was in an episode of the Twilight Zone; it was unbelievable and very unprofessional, they had the Beverly Hillbillies in the management positions, you can tell by some of the management decisions they were making. My brother ended up retiring soon after all the above stuff went down; I never heard from him after he retired. Have you heard enough yet? Well, I have more so let's move on to the next bit of crap.

PERVERT CENTRAL

During my twenty years of employment and my approximately fifty-six years of life at this time; I thought I had seen a lot in my life, I thought I had already seen the good, bad and the ugly. Boy was I wrong! I soon realized I still had not seen all the freaky shit, I was to see in my life.

This next incident to cross my path was something I will carry with me the rest of my life; I will never forget this moment in my life, it will be with me like remembering the first time you threw up after drinking, a bad car accident you may have been in, an happy or unhappy situation that happen in your life, an unbelievable incident that you just cannot shake, every time you close your eyes you have to open them again.

This happen within the last five years of my employment with in the So-Low CSD; the CSD was a division of the DA's office, the director of our office was Tim, he had held the Director's position for approximately eight years prior to this incident happening.

Almost every day at work I ate sunflower seeds at my desk; it was just a habit I had, what's funny is outside of work I would not eat a sunflower seed, not one. When this incident happens, I had been working in my position for approximately fifteen years; they give you merit raise every year, I was at the top of my pay scale currently, but top pay of the scale still wasn't shit.

I was doing my regular CS job and I was also going to court and representing the office in court, I believe it was every fourth Monday for about ten to fifteen years I had to go to court and handle different legal issue that can arise within a case in the CSD, I would deal with anywhere from five to fifteen cases every time I appeared in court.

That's right, I was not good enough to be a supervisor, but I was good enough to represent the So-Low in the court of law, I am not an attorney, I did things like take the custodial and non-custodial parents in to a room and conduct a mediation or I would depose one or both parents and try to get them to come to an amicable agreement, I would do DNA testing on possible fathers, I would deal with all types of issue going on in people lives, I would deal with mental issues between parents. We had CS Assistance in court producing all the necessary documents we needed, it would be attorneys, a couple CS officers and a couple of CS assistance in the court room, along with the court clerks, court stenographer, bailiff, and judge.

Every day at the end of each day at approximately four fourth-five each day; I would start getting ready to leave to go home, I kept a tube of toothpaste and a toothbrush in my desk. I would go in the restroom, and I will use the bathroom and brush my teeth before I left each day this was a regular routine for me as long as I had been employed at So-Low CSD.

I would sometime run into different guys in the restroom; this particular day I went on my routine restroom visit, I walked in the restroom the Director of the CSD was standing in the restroom with his drawls down on his ankles looking at himself in the mirror in front of him, he was not standing in the stall, he was standing outside of the stall, he did not try to pull his drawls up real quick when I walked in, he was just standing there admiring himself in the mirror in front of him. What you have to understand is he is a white man that stood about five feet eleven inches tall approximately three fifty to four hundred pounds, his stomach hung all over his junk from my angel it look like two blueberries and one green grape tucked in a canyon, it looked like a snake head and it's body stuck under a large boulder, it looked like a bad car wreck, it took everything I had to hold my food down.

When I walked in, I looked at him and I said "what the fuck"! I threw my hands not over my head but straight out to my sides; he turned his head to the right and looked at me in the eyes and smiled, then turned his head back toward the mirror, then he turned his head back toward me looked me in the eyes and smile again. I said Tim "What the fuck", again! He turned his head back toward the mirror, he turned his head and looked at me in the eyes again and smile at me then he turned his head back toward the mirror in front of him again. I looked at him as he looked at himself in the mirror, he turned his head toward me and looking at me in the eyes again and smiled, I said "What the Fuck" again!! Then he turned his head back to his mirror then turned his head toward me looked me in the eyes again and smile at me again, I looked at him and said "What the Fuck again"!!! He just was continuing the same motion, each time I said WHAT THE FUCK!!!!!! I said it with more emotion each time he looked at me. I finally said Tim you have gone Fucking Crazy!! It was some of the creepiest shit I had ever experience.

I did not have my cell phone on me, I left in my office charging for my ride home. If I would have had my cell phone on me, I would have had that big old bitch walking round that bathroom like he was on the runway for Vogue Magazine, I would have had that fat motherfucker prancing round like he was in a musical. I was pissed that I did not have my cell phone on me.

So, I decided not to take a piss; it was no way I was going to touch my pants in anyway, I was not unbuckling my belt, pants and was not going to unzip my pants, I was not going to give this fool any ideals. The way the restroom is set up, you walk down a hallway, then you enter the restroom to your left as you enter the restroom there is three sinks about a foot or two apart from each other, each sink has a mirror above it, when the door close behind me there are two urinals to your left and

89

one toilet stall that sit to the right of the urinals, one sink is directly in front of the stall that is where he was standing, I was standing in front of the sink nearest to the door there was a sink in between our sinks. I decide to brush my teeth while he was standing there with his drawls down, I could not believe this was happening, I was in shock! I thought about whooping his fat ass! That is what the younger version of me would have done, that would have gotten my ass thrown in jail, because it would have been his word against mine. The Director of the CSD, an Attorney, he had more years with So-Low then I did, he is white man, in a majority white county. Yeah, if I would have kicked his ass. I would be locked up as we speak. So, I decided to brush my teeth to see how long he was going to stand there; this motherfucker stood there while I brushed my teeth. I was stand to the side so he could not run up behind me; I had my booty pressed again the door, after I finish brushing my teeth. I said you are crazier than motherfucker! I told him I am going to report him; he started pulling up his pants then I walked out of the restroom, the first person I encountered was Cubicle Etiquette she was walking toward the break room. I told her right then because she was my supervisor at the time, she seen him leaving the restroom, he left after me, I told her what happen at the entrance of the break room so she could still see down the hallway. She responded by saying Harry, I do not want to hear that; I told her you are my supervisor. I suppose to report it to you, she said that is too much information for me and walked off.

The way I looked at this incident is he had to go! You cannot be a pervert and be the director of the CSD. All the kids that be around the CSD, there are parents and kids around all the time. My coworkers picked up their kids from school and bring them to work all the time; it has been many time I walked in the restroom and saw one of my co-workers son's in the restroom, if one of those young man would have walked in the restroom when I did that could have been devastating and could have cause mental issues with that child for the rest of his life or he could have done worst and tried to molest the child or have the child play with him after all it shocked the hell out of me! My stomach still get upset every time I think about it. He looked like a giant steam pork bun; I thought I had seen everything in my life until then, I grew up in the Bay Area, I saw a man get shot, I saw drug addicts laying there with a needle still in their arm, I had a gun pointed and shot in my direction, I seen all types of shit in my life. I had never seen a pervert in action he is a pervert because anyone that would do what he did could not be in his right mind.

After I told cubicle etiquette; I started telling all my co-workers, some was surprised at his actions, some was not at all, I told them to watch their son's when they go to the restroom, I told them to at least walk their son to the door do not send them to the restroom by themselves. Some of my co-workers was surprised and some was not. I thought he was a good director until this incident; this incident spoiled what little bit of respect I had for him, I did not talk to him daily I would talk to him in passing only, his office was across the building from my office. He did not come out his office and walk around and talk to his employee; the only time we would hear from him is at an all-staff meeting, he would show up and talk about any changes that is happening, then he would go back to his office. I hope he was not staying in his office jacking off, he had plenty of time by himself, a one man shows playing with his one-eyed monster, I can go on and on with this one.

Approximately two weeks before this incident happen; he had chosen the person he was grooming to succeed him, her name was Rhonda, yeah, she is blond hair blue eyes, she's a nice looking middle aged white woman married with a couple kids at home. For the short period of time, I knew her, she was a nice person; I did not tell her about the incident for another two or three weeks, I did not want to drop a bomb like that on her as she was being trained by him. I did not know if she was ready for something like that. I continued to tell others in the office; I did not care; I figured the more the merrier.

Two or three weeks later; I decided to tell Rhonda our replacement director about the incident, she told me to go tell our lead attorney about it and see what he says. His name Brett, I walked down to his office; asked if he had a minute to talk, he was cool he had been there for about year, he came over from the criminal division he was the lead attorney over there. We got along good he lived in Bob, California, the area Tree-landers did not like, he was a sports fan like me, matter of fact he was the person who got my phone line back. He would call my office extension and get this number is not in service; we had worked on many cases together during the one-year period he had worked in the CSD, we would laugh and talk mess because he was born on the east coast, and I was born on the west coast. I believe he was born outside of the Boston area; he was a Patriot and Red Sox fan; I was Raider and A's fan. He would call my office, and he would get this line is not in service recording every time he called me; he knew I was in the office because he would have talk to me or he would have heard me talking in my office. He walked over to my office and said Harry why can't I call your office? I told him management took my phone line away from me over two years ago. I told him they just gave me my office back right before he transferred over here; I told him I have not had a direct phone line for at least the past four to five years. He said wait a minute! You are one of our top collectors; I said I know, he said how could you be a top collector and you do not have an incoming direct line, I told him when they took my direct phone line away I made sure when I notated my cases, the officer who received my clients call back would know exactly what my next steps was to collect the support that way I did not always have to take the call myself, he said smart, I told him I always adapt and overcome. He said Well, I am going to get your line back, I told him thanks.

So back to me telling him about Tim. I said Brett you know Tim. He said yes, I said you two are good friends, he said yes, we are pretty good friends. I said well your good friend was doing perverted acts in the restroom he said, No Way! I said Yeah Way! I told him I worked for this man for approximately ten years now; I have never come up with something like this about him. He said I been to Tim's house and my son, I told him do not leave your son alone with him, I could tell he was stunned by what I was telling him his complexion was plush red when I left; they also knew I would not just make this shit up. I guess he went back and talk to Rhonda about our conversation. I ended up getting a portion of my phone line back. I still had some restrictions, but for the most part I had it back I could get a call from an extension in the office; but not a direct call from the public, they still had to go through the switchboard.

I told Rhonda one day while we were passing, I want to have a meeting with Tim; she said she will try to set the meeting up, about four weeks went by and I have not heard a word from Rhonda. Then one day out of the blue with no time to prepare; Rhonda stopped by my office and said if I want my meeting, now is the time. She said he got time for me right now, the last four weeks he was not doing anything but sit in his office, I knew when he was in the building, his office was right across the building from my office and his door was always closed.

So, I got up and grabbed a couple pens and paper; I started walking with Rhonda back to Tim and Rhonda office, I realized I forgot something, I ran back to my office and grabbed my little Sony recorder. Rhonda looked at me and said what is in your hands? I told her this is my digital recorder from when I worked at a prior law firm; we walked into Tim's office, he was sitting behind his big desk. I was sitting on the other side of his desk; Rhonda was sitting to my right at this little round table with four chairs.

I looked across the desk at Tim, he was looking at me like he was going to intimidate me, I had been there, done that, I had set in deposition with many stiff shirts both male and female, I worked at a law firm prior to holding the CS position. We recorded the date and all the members that was present at the meeting. I asked him if he wanted to start, he said you are blaming me for something, you start. I said OK; I said do you remember on the date of 7/20/16 at approximately four forty-five pm, I walk in the upstairs bathroom and you were stand in the restroom with your pants and underwear down on your ankles where any and every one who walked in could see you looking at yourself in the mirror. He said was it four forty-five or four forty? I said you know what I am talking about. He said no I don't because it never happens. I said are you on any medication then you might have an excuse for your odd behavior. He said I do not know what incident you are talking about, he also said he was not taking medication. I told him that was a perverted act I witness in the restroom, I asked him was he waiting for someone, he said I was waiting for you, I told him you were not waiting for me, then I said, if you were waiting for me, I would not be going to report your ass to the police. I told him I will go to the police, newspapers, his superiors, and CPS. He said if you want to pugnacious; I really did not know what pugnacious meant, I figure it meant I was getting ready to report his perverted ass to the police, then yeah, I was pugnacious. I told him if he does not come clean, I was going to file a police report today, right after I leave this office, he said he cannot come clean because he did not do anything, I told him I gave you an out with the medication offer, you said you are not on medication. I gave you a chance to come clean and you lied. I said I am wasting my time here; I am going to my supervisor's office, and I am going to tell her I must leave right now; I am going to drive straight to the Police Department, and I am going to file a formal complaint against you right now! I start to get out my chair and he yelled if you leave this office right now! You will not be coming back again!!! He said you better not leave this building!! I believe this was a Thursday afternoon at about three thirty when the meeting came to an end; the meeting lasted for about an hour and a half, it was about three thirty when he was threating my job. Tim should have been terminated for threating my job; he cannot threaten my job when the complaint involved him, so he was no longer my superior. Rhonda heard every word of our meeting; she did not say a word I believe all parties in the meeting had their recorders set and recording. I did not leave work early, I left work at five in the evening, I called in sick the next day on Friday I wanted him to think I was going to report him that day, but I took the day off and relaxed my mind. I was late to work on the following Monday morning which is when I reported him to the Police Department, Monday morning approximately eight thirty. They had me waiting for approximately twenty minutes before an office came out; I told him I wanted to report an incident that happen at my place of employment, I told him I work for the So-Low CSD. I told him about the incident, and I wanted to file an official complaint against him; I said this man freaked me out when I saw him standing there like he was on a runway, I said to myself: "Tim has gone crazy". He said he will have an officer stop by my job and take my report, the officer came by the next day around one o'clock in the afternoon. They page me over the loudspeaker because I was on my phone when they tried to call me; I called receptionist after I hung up the phone and they told me a police officer was there to talk to me.

I came downstairs to the receptionist area and introduce myself to the officer; he introduces himself to me and gave me his business card we stepped outside in the parking lot by his patrol car, he took my report

I asked him if he wanted me to take him into the building, I can show you the crime scene, he said no that is alright! I said to myself they are not going to do shit, I said what are you planning to do? He said we will have the report entered in their system and if he does anything else like this, we will pick him up. I asked the officer do he know how many kids be in and out of our building every today. I said to the officer is the Police Department going to continue to let a pervert be the director of the CSD, he said it is his word against mine, I played the recording I had of our meeting, he was convinced Tim was lien, but he still did not do anything but file the report, I said you not even going to investigate the incident. He said no, I am going to file the report. I said OK. I said thanks, for nothing to myself! I did not know why I thought he was going to do something at least question him about the incident; it was a white officer but what would I expect in this town. They might have had one or two Mexican officers, no Black officers for sure on the force. I had worked about fifteen years at this time. I have not seen a Black on the police force or with the So-Low Sheriff Department there you go again, the good ole boy network at his best, if you are not white then you are not right, in this county white privilege at its best.

I was determine to get rid of him; I took an oath at the beginning of my employment with So-Low to report any type of sexual misconduct to the elderly, women, children or me, what he did was a sick act, I told myself, I will contact the newspaper and see if they was willing to talk to me or write a story about the incident. I called the Tree-land Gazette and spoke to a reporter; he listens to the incident and asked a few questions, he said he will talk it over with a few co-workers, editors, and mangers, he said he will get back to me and let me know if they were going to carry the story. After about two weeks, I called him because I had not heard from him. I had to leave a message I called again a few days later with no answer, I had to leave another message. I never received a call back from Mr. Harris. Another example of the good ole boy network at his best. I contact the Sacramento Newspaper; they never got back to me I left a message on one of their general recorders stating there is a Pervert running the CSD in So-Low asking if they can please contact me at my number, I never heard from anyone with that paper.

So I turned to the state agency for about the fourth time looking for justice; this time I set an appointment to go see the state agency located in the bay area, I took off work and went to the Fremont, California office I spoke to African American Representative his name was Mr. Jones he took me into his office, we set down for about an hour I told him about the incident and how it happen. He said Tim was trying to sexually harass me; I said to him "What you talking about Willis"? I said wait a minute what are you talking about sexual harass me? Mr. Jonas said, the reason he was trying to harass me, because he continued to stand there after I walked in the restroom. He was waiting to see if you were going to do something; I told Mr. Jonas, I was not going to do shit! I told him I thought about kicking his fat ass; Mr. Jonas said good thing you did not do that; then you would have been in jail, he said he would have said you walked in the bathroom and beat him up. He said did you have your phone? I said no, I said I wish I had it, it was on the charger in my office. I told him I was pissed I did not have it on me.

I asked him if I could file my complaint in the Fremont office; he said he wish he could help me in his office, I must take the case to Sacramento office because it is closest to your place of employment. I told him I been to the Sacramento office; I will be honest with you, I really wish I can have my case transferred to Fremont office or Oakland office, he asked why you want case transferred to our office so bad, I told him I had to go to the Sacramento office about three times prior on So-Low because of their misconduct. He said what other misconducts; I explained the other issues he said you had good reason to seek help, he said Sacramento office should have assist you also, he said he was sorry the Sacramento office must handle the case. I told him about every time I went to the Sacramento office, I got a Mexican Representative who is scared to actually help people, they are just happy to be getting a pay check. I told him just like in my office; I had talked to every Mexican representative in my office; they are all mad because they are working every day and being passed over for promotions, I use to tell them if they all stuck together they can make changes in our office, they was all scared and did not want to make waves, that was both male and female Mexican representatives, they continued to be by passed for promotion, they was just happy to get a check every two weeks, respect was one thing they were scared to go after. That is what the Mexican representatives at Sacramento state agency did with my prior cases; they went through the motions then close my cases, maybe they worked harder for the Mexican clients, all I know is they did not do shit for me.

I am not into suing companies; I am also not in to being missed treated in any working environment, there is harassment and discrimination law protecting the company employees and protecting tenants housing discrimination laws. These laws were entered to stop any mistreatment of employees or people looking for fair housing; it is the Civil Rights Division of Laws for the state of California, their principle responsibility is to enforce all Civil Rights Laws. This division was implemented to protect the people of California from unlawful employment, housing, unsafe public accommodations, hate violence and even human trafficking. Sacramento office of this state agency failed me terribly, the head representative of this state agency was an Asian woman, I contact her on many occasions, I left messages for her to get back to me; she called me back and told me to continue the process. As you can imagine; I was terribly disappointed when I left the Fremont office. I came home and started working on how I was going to get the

98

office to help me, I could not afford an attorney. My family and I was living above water, we were not financially stable enough where I can take three thousand to ten thousand dollars to retain an attorney. This African American attorney in San Francisco; I went and met with him in this nice high-rise office in this building on Market Street which is right downtown San Francisco, when I entered the office and was looking around, I notice he had four white male assistance working for him, they was bring him coffee, taking calls, bring him his files and documents. One white representative ask me if I want something to drink while I was waiting to meet with the attorney; he brought me a water, they had nice antiques furniture in the office, when I met with the attorney he told me he was willing to take my case, but he wanted ten thousand dollars down to retain his services, I said I wanted to retain him, not buy him. I asked would he consider taking my case pro-bono basis; he started talking about the distance he would have to travel to represent me he told me he could not represent me on a pro-bono basis. I told him I cannot afford him; I said thanks for your time and consideration we went our separate ways, I interviewed with a couple other attorney's but was not successful with retaining their services.

This meant I had to depend on Sacramento state agency to do their job; I was hoping I did not get the same representative. I filed the intake package with the state agency; I was not feeling comfortable because I had filed at least three other complaints against So-Low because of prior mistreatments experienced. In my prior cases I brought forth to this state agency; I had dates, times, written documents, emails, in order. I tried to present the case as professional as possible, I had to keep returning to the agency because of So-Low mistreatment of me. I tried to make my case as professional as possible; I also tried to keep my cases as elementary as possible. You heard the mistreatment I was receiving doing my years of employment with So-Low; how would you feel if you were mistreatment like I was? The agency took my case they assigned my case to a representative last name Moreno which is a representative who had assisted me on two other prior cases; I was really disappointed; I ask her are you going to help me this time or are you going to swipe my case up under the rug again. I told her I am not the type of person who like suing companies; I said but I refuse to have a company continue to mistreat me also.

No company should disrespect their employees to the level So-Low CSD has treated me; if you are not white, you are not right. I met with the state representative and talked over the phoned; she want to give me a right to sue letter again, meaning I have the right to go get me an attorney, see before you can sue a company, you have to go through this state agency to get a right to sue letter, this letter give you permission to sue a company or not give you permission to sue. That is the agency way of sweeping your case up under the rug they gave me a right to sue letter on all my cases; this case I was determined to not let them brush me off again.

Back to Tim, I was calling him (Pervert Central) by this time, I was not going to have that motherfucker around all those children that goes in and out of our building on a daily basis. I always wondered why Pervert Central use to drive his mobile home to work all the time; I guess since he only had to walk from the building to his camper it gave him more time to jack off at twelve noon. I thought he was just driving the camper to start it and run it for a while; for what I understand he only lived about five miles from the office, it seems to me starting it, backing it out and parking it would take more time then driving it to the office. I never paid any attention to Pervert Central and his camper until after the restroom incident; then he was trussed to the forefront of my thinking, I was not obsessed with him, but I wanted to get him for what he did. He had to go! In my book the incident was just not cool, his action did not sit well with me, I could no longer look at him as a man; he made me sick to my stomach.

I told state representative she will not give me a right to sue letter, I told her she is going to do her job this time, I said if she doesn't stop my mistreatment, I told her I will go over her head and I mention the Asian CEO of the state agency. I told her she is the reason why I am back here every year; because you are not doing anything to stop my mistreatment. She said why you won't look for a new place of employment. I said why do I have to look for a new place of employment? I told her if you did your job I would not have to work in a hostile environment; I asked her do she know how to do her job? She said yes, I said well do your job and stop So-Low from fucking with me whenever they feel like it! I told her So-Low will never stop their garbage until you stop it! I yelled at her to do your job!

I insisted on a formal hearing concerning this restroom incident; I told her I will continue to go over her head until she do her job, I ask for her supervisor and managers name and phone numbers. I called the head of the state agency at the time and spoke to the CEO; we were on first name basis after a while, we had a meeting and went over my case I told her everything that happen, I also told her this incident had me freaked out! I could not get the incident out of my mind; that shit tripped me out! Teri was force to grant me a mediation hearing; she hired a mediation representative a white women blonde hair blues eyes, what else, I asked her are you going to treat me fair, she stated she always treated all parties equal, she said she is always impartial third party in the negotiation, she is there to make sure both parties are treated equal, she will use her law degree and her negotiation skill to come to a fair and impartial resolution between the two parties and the conflict at hand. I asked her again if she was going to treat me fair; I told her all that legal mumbo jumbo do not mean a thing if she is not going to be fair. I asked her was she contacted by the county or the State Agency, she stated the state agency hired her.

We met at the office of agency in their conference room; I was the only one sitting on my said of the table, the county had a little Spanish woman representing them and Pervert Central, Rhonda was there also. I really do not know why she came to the mediation; I guess since she was in the initial meeting between Pervert Central and I, that is the only reason I felt she was present.

When the meeting started, we started talking about a case I brought forth a couple years ago, I told the Mary the mediator we are not here for this case, I told her we are here for restroom incident. I looked Mary and said thanks for being fair. She stated we will deal with the restroom incident; they was talk about the Mercedes incident which have already been taking care of when they suspended me for two weeks without pay, they was also talking about anything else they could come up with, I told Mary before we left for lunch she lied to me, I told her she led me to believe I was going to get a fair shake, but instead she lied. She stated when we return from lunch, we will deal with the restroom incident. I said OK, we will see.

After lunch So-Low Attorney wanted to question me; she asked several questions one of the questions was have I ever been called the N word while working at So-Low CSD. I told her I am sure I have been called a nigger daily; but not to my face or out loud, I told her about the incident at the fairgrounds. I told her, I can tell how some people look at me they are calling me a nigger. I don't know how many times I was walking down a hallway and one of the co-workers said Harry you scared me! When they finally realized I was walking down the same hallway, they said they could not see me because the hall was dark, for all I know that could have been their way of calling me a nigger.

As the little female Hispanic Attorney continued to question me

Pervert Central kept trying to interrupt me, the little female attorney kept telling him to be quiet, Pervert Central kept trying to stop me from talking, finally, the attorney just looked at him and told him to shut up! Don't say another word! Else I will have you sit outside of this deposition, he finally shut up after that. I asked if I would get to question Pervert Central; they did not want to let me do that, the Hispanic attorney said no I started asking Pervert Central questions anyway, his attorney started tell him not to answer. I looked at Mary the mediator and she stated well his attorney is refusing for her client to answer my questions. I said Mary, how are you going to be able to make a ruling when she is not allowing Pervert Central to answer my questions, I told them Pervert Central violated my employment rights when he threaten to terminate me in the meeting I attended with him and Rhonda, I told Rhonda and Pervert Central I was going to the police and he told me I am not going anywhere, if I do I was not coming back again, since the complaint was against him, he was no longer my superior, he was my equal, so he did not have the right to threaten me with termination of my job, his attorney said that is not correct! Mary said she heard enough; I told her I have not heard enough. I said what are you talking about you heard enough? It was starting to get late and heated; it was about three thirty in the evening and I was pissed! They wanted to make me an offer; I asked what type of offer? Mary said let me talk to So-Low's attorney ; they want to step out of the office and negotiated, I said I believe I am a party to the action, So-Low attorney got upset when I did not allow them to leave the room. She stated we will give you one year pay and I must leave my position; I said to the Attorney and Mediator you are kidding right? You rather pay me one year pay, have me leave my position and keep the pervert, I said somehow that does not sound right. I was thinking, "white pervert privilege at its best". (I said that to myself). She stated that is all she authorized to approve; I told her she must make a better offer then that, I told her my pain and suffering is worth more then what they are offering, I said, I have been through hell with this unprofessional ass company, I plan to work at least twenty years, it was around my seventeenth year of employment at this time. So-Low attorney was trying her best to get out of the meeting; she was saying she will talk to So-Low Administrative Representative Department Head and get back to me, Helen is the head administrated representative who told me she had to take my full check instead of letting me pay the unfair penalty back in payments.

I said can you call your client; she said I need to talk to them in person, she asked me what do I want? I told her I want to be treated fairly; I want the offer to be equivalent to the suffering I had been subjected too over the years. I want to be paid equivalent to the systemic racism I have received over my years with So-Low, I also want Pervert Central to be terminated and relieved of his position immediately, we cannot have a pervert running the CSD, I said do you realize how many kids come in and out of the CSD a day, I told them there is hundreds of kids walk in our office a week with their parents, I asked can the CSD afford the cost of a missing child because of this idiot, I said my co-workers bring their kids in the building after school when needed, I said So-Low CSD rather keep the pervert then me, I took an oath for this very reason to report perverts. I went to the newspapers, the police department, the administrations, the union and the state agency that was suppose too protect me and the kids, they all are refusing to do anything to rectify the problem; none of you are doing anything to stop it. The children and I said thanks a lot! You should be a shame of yourself, you guys are fantastic! So-Low Attorney and the Mediator was ready to go after I said this to them, Rhonda was there and heard me also but did not say a word, they all knew I was right. They could not argue with me; I told the mediator I was disappointed by the way she handles the mediation, I told the Attorney I will be looking forward to her call in the near future.

She called back about a week later told me they negotiated for Pervert Central to leave at the end of the year which was approximately ninety days until Christmas; he also will use some of his vacation in between the date we talked and the end of the year. She asked me on the days Pervert Central is in the build will I be willing to go downstairs to use the restroom on the first floor, she said because of Pervert Central physical condition, I said hell no! I said what is his physical condition dropping his drawls in the middle of restrooms for everyone to see, he was overweight and use to sweat like a pig, we was on the second floor at this time, I told the attorney I am not comfortable with him in the building, I am in hostile and unsafe environment, I told her I do not give a damn about his physical condition, I can go to any restroom, I am not going to make any special concession for him, he has to go down stairs to use the restroom. I told her we have a women restroom, a men restroom, and the pervert restroom is the downstairs restroom. He had to go downstairs my female co-workers was laughing at him behind his back; they would see him going to the downstairs restroom struggling and sweating like a stuff pig. Everyone was asking me what happen in my deposition; I told a couple co-workers about the restroom agreement, he had to retire by the end of the year that is all I told them. I knew what I told my co-workers was going to fly through the grapevine in the office. I only had to tell one or two people and the rest of the office would know. What can I say? It was office full of woman.

They offer me two years pay to leave So-Low, I need about five years pay, I also wanted five years of work credited toward my retirement which would had taken me over the twenty years of service. I need about three years at the time. But five years would have given me more money in my pocket and would have taken my retirement to the year twenty-twenty two. The attorney told me Helen, stated they would give me the two years, but I must waive my retirement, you see what type of mentality I am dealing with. They want me to give up double digit years of service for two years of pay; the mediation representative did exactly what they always done, nothing! The state agency told me if I turned down their offer then they were not going to interfere any longer. I could not take the offer because it was not in my best interest for my family and myself. I would lose my medical coverage for my family and myself. I wanted them to add three years of medical coverage to the deal and I told them I would take the deal. So-Low's attorney said she asked Helen, and she stated two years of pay, no medical coverage. So, I stated on the job and waited until the next bullshit to cross my path. It was coming and soon. Pervert Central ended up retiring at the end of the year I believe it was end of twenty-sixteen; he would sometime show his face around office, he and I would have words if I saw him. I told Rhonda our new director I did not feel comfortable with him in the building; when he is in the building I am in a hostile and unsafe environment, I will be forced to file another complaint with our union and state agency if he continues to come into the building after our agreement, he was to retired. So, Rhonda told him they would have to communicate through email, or by phone. Our Union Local 39 in Sacramento was not worth mentioning; they are so deep in So-Low pocket, our Union Representative was sucking the counties dick through a hold in their pocket, it was a waste of time and money. I stopped seeing Pervert Central in the building after that point. I would still see Pervert Central around town from time to time; he would not approach me or say anything to me because we were no longer in the office, he was not going to get out of line in a public venue I was just glad Pervert Central was no longer in the office.

RHONDA

believe Rhonda was surprised to see how I handle myself in the pressure environment; she also believes the women in our office had a certain amount of respect for me, they would look up to me because I was older and at this time, I was a pretty seasoned officer, I would also talk shit to the women from time to time to keep them in a good mood. I knew if I kept them in a good mood the days would go better, and they would help me if I needed help with something. She also liked me because I was one of the few officers that was not afraid to go to her office and just have a conversation with her. She like that about me, because all the other officers would not go anywhere near her office, unless they were called to the office. She called me one day and asked me to come to her office, she stated she want to talk to me about something, when I arrive to her office she asked me to sit down. She said Harry you been employed here for quite some time; I told her yes! I had been there about seventeen years now. She said you have always been one of our top collectors, she asked me have I ever been interested in becoming a supervisor. I told her I already been there done that! I told her I been bypassed more times than a fat woman on the hoe stroll; I said the only thing I want is some peace of mind, that is all I am asking for is peace of mind, I said I want everyone off my nerves. I have a few more years of work here and I plan to retire from this office within the next three years. They had me schedule to leave in twenty-twenty two; there was no way I could have stated there that long, I was not man enough, I would have beat the shit out of one of those women if I would have stayed that long.

Rhonda said that is too bad; she wanted to ask me to apply for the next supervisor position that came available, she felt I could really help her with a lot of the women she was having difficulty with; the majority of the women in the office was not making it easy for her to adjust, they was talking pretty bad about her behind her back and questioning her authority they did not agree with her new policies she was trying to implement.

I remember one time we were having a staff meeting Rhonda was running it, this was the first time she was running the meeting in our office; some of the more experience officers was trying to make it as difficult as possible for her to give her ideas, strategy and suggestions, they kept debating her on her Ideas and suggestions. She was starting to get frustrated; she looked like she was getting ready to cry, I remember sitting in the meeting thinking to myself young lady whatever you do, do not started crying in this meeting, because they would have her right where they want her, she did not cry thank God, by her not crying showed she had pretty tough skin, I told her I appreciate the consideration for the supervisor position. I told her if she still need help with my co-workers; I will help her by talking to my co-workers about giving her a fair chance. She said thanks a lot for assisting her with some of the more difficult employees; I told her to let me know who she is having the most problems with, I will go and try to talk to them or at least try to get them to give her a fair shot in earning their trust. I told her if one of her problems is an older representative and close to retirement; why try to change them now, just let them retire. I told her she can fill those vacancies with people she can train to be the type of officer she want them to be, there was about five officers that was nearing retirement, all the others officers I will talk too whomever she like me too, the other co-workers would not have known she had asked me to talk to them, Rhonda would go through the chain of command first before she asked me to talk to them, some supervisors was younger then I and less experience dealing with the others rather they was employees or clients. I know she did not come to my rescue in the meeting with Pervert Central, the state agency and the mediator, but she could have picked a side and made it worse for me, she kept quit and stayed out of it and that was cool with me.

THE STOCKER

This is something I always thought I would only see on the television; this young lady was as crazy as a woman can get, I received a call from a co-worker asking me to handle a case for her, she said Harry, I have a black woman in my caseload and she is driving me crazy, I told my co-worker to tell the custodial parent I will call her back, she wanted to hold for me. Our calls could last anywhere from five minutes to an hour or more depending on what issues you are dealing with; the custodial parent is the parent who has the child most of the time, in this particular relationship the mother was the custodial parent, her name was Kathy. I told my co-worker to tell her I will call her back; I called her back about an hour later, she was the mother of a little boy about the age of six, she and her son's live in an apartment in one of the towns outside of So-Low just north of the county. She had a pretty good job working for a city or the state near her home; I called her and we started discussing her case, she was more than happy to give me whatever info I asked her for, and even info I did not ask for, she was also trying to get as much info as she could about me, I made sure I was keeping my info to myself, I kept telling her this case is about you not me, she continue to talk to me about their relationship and how she got pregnant. She stated she met a young Black man; he told her how much he liked her, and was telling her how fine she looks, she stated he took her to dinner a couple times, she said they went to Applebee's and Chevy's, after they had dinner at Chevy's we went back to his car, I asked her what type of car he droves, she said he had a Cadillac. I said what year Cadillac? She said it is an older model and it had a couple dents in body and this grey colored paint, I said is the car grey or primer, she said it was not painted

110

it was primer, I asked her if she knew the difference between primer and paint, she said she is not sure of the difference, I told her paint will shine more the primer, I said primer does not shine like paint, I explained primer is the under coat, she said the car was primer. They drove off and before he took her to her parent's home, he pulled over and he talked her into the back seat, they climb in the back seat and made love as she put it! I have other words for it, I will keep the word to myself, they end up Fuckin a couple times in the back seat and she got pregnant. She missed her period, called him, told him she was pregnant, he hung up the phone on her, from that point on he stopped accepting her calls, she later found out he had six other children from a bunch of other women, when I started working on his background search, I discovered he did not have a background, he had criminal record, no work history at all, he sold dope, he lived off women who would let him sleep with them or sleep on their couch, he had women in other counties who had been trying to get money out of him for years. I took the phone numbers she had for him and told her I will contact her in a couple days, I said give me time to review and work her case, fifteen minutes later I received another call from her, she stated she had more info to give me, I said what info do you have, she gave me the names and numbers to reach a couple of his other babies momma's. I said thanks, I asked her is that all the information you have. She said yes, I said I will talk to you in a couple days, this girl continues to call me all day; she must have called me ten times each day, I tried calling the father of her kid, he did not recognize my number, he answered one of my phone calls. I explained to him who I was and why I was calling; he stated he was trapped into this relationship and he was not going to pay child support for their child, he stated she told him she was on birth control, I told him that is the oldest trick in the book, he said I do not know if that child is his, he said I fucked her in the back seat of my car, he said what type of woman will get pregnant in the back seat of the car, I told him the type of woman who will climb back there with him, he said she is nothing but a whore, he said I will never pay that bitch shit, I hate that bitch. I told him young man this child support is going to ruin his life if he does not deal with it; he said my life is already ruin, I told him he will never have anything in life, he will eventually have to look this problem in the eye and take care of it. I told him as he get older he's going to want something out of life and this child support will come back and bite him in his behind; I told him I will guarantee he will regret this decision, he stated he hate that bitch, he said she is going to drive me crazy, she will be calling me all day, every day like she has been calling him, he said she is one of the worst people he knows, he said I will find out just what type of person she is, he said he hate that bitch and hung up on me. He proceeds to change his number to his cell phone because the next time I called him the number was no longer in service.

She continue to call me approximately ten times a day, she was starting to drive me crazy like he told me, she would continue to call me on my direct line and she call the receptionist area, they would answer the line and transfer the call to me directly and I would answer my line, and some time I would not answer my line, I would let it go to my voice mail, most of the time I would let it go to voice mail because this woman act like her case was the only case I had to work. She would call sometimes and just want to talk to me about the father and their short relationship and she said she started to fall in love with him and how he misled her. She stated he told her he loved her, and he enjoyed being with her when they were talking on the phone and at dinner. He filled her head with all this lovey-dovey bullshit and she felled for it hook line and sinker, even to the point that she dropped her guard and underwear, she started crying. I told her to stop crying; I told her I cannot work your case if I am on the phone with her all the time, I told her I must hang up, because I have other cases and work to do, she would continue to talk on the phone. I told her I have to get off the line, while I am talking to her I might have a walk in, another phone call or I might have a call backs that I have to make some time, I started hanging up on her ass when I got tire of talking to her, sometime it just had to be done that way, she refuse to hang up the phone. She started calling and giving me different address where non-custodial parent was living; I would send our investigator out to serve him to get him into court, she gave me about four different addresses all of them was wrong. I road with our investigator a couple times he was a cool brother with long and thick dreadlocks, he was a brother who worked as an independent process server and private investigator. He would spy on husbands, wives, and other family members; he would secretly follow people and take photographs of people's husband and wives cheating on each other, I would tell him he investigated people's privates, we use to laugh. We went pass one of the addresses and a woman answer the door, she stated she just threw him out a couple of days ago, we asked her if she knew where he went, she said he is staying with another one of his whores or might be stating in his car, she said she does not give damn about where he went as long as his ass is out of her apartment, she called him a broke ass motherfucker! I continue to work with the custodial parent, and she continue to drive me nuts with all her phone calls; most of the time I did not accept her calls she would continue to call approximately ten times a day. Our switchboard representatives would call and tell me my favor client is calling, it would be eight thirty in the morning, I started telling them to decline her calls. I handle anywhere from eight to ten thousand case in my case load alone; sometimes I would have our receptionist patch the call through and I would try my best to make her understand her case was not the only case I handled, then she wants to just talk about her life and she never having any money because we are not collecting on her case. I would tell her she need to stop calling me all the time, I told her you call every ten to fifteen minutes constantly every day, she would be calling from her work phone and on her cell phone, I told her she do not give us enough time to work her case because she is constantly calling my office, I told her do not call me for at least a week, the bitch called fifteen minutes later. I told my reception not to put her call through to me for at least a week; after two days of calling, she called and cursed out our receptionist; when she finally got me on the phone after three days of cursing out our receptionist, she asks me was I the only black person in the building, I said yes, why? She asked what time you go to lunch, I told her I do not go to lunch until late afternoon, she said do you go at a certain time, I said no, just late afternoon, she said can she come take me to lunch, I said hell no, I am not going to lunch with your ass, she continue to ask me to go to lunch during our conversation on the phone, I continue to tell her no! I felt she was young, stupid and I could not go to lunch with her even if I wanted too, and I did not want too.

One day she decided to take off work and stake my office out; she set in her car and waited until I left for lunch one day, I walked out of our building about two thirty and she was parked across the street in the same parking lot, I always parked my car in. It was In Shape gym who moved in the building across the street from me at this time; I walked across the street, got in my car and drove approximately four blocks from my place of employment and parked my car, she followed me to the restaurant and parked the next row over, I did not see her following me, I seen her get out of her car as I was getting out of my car, I started to walk over to the restaurant entrance she is walking about ten feet behind me, I grabbed the door handle and held the door for her to walk in she was alright looking, her breast was big she had a low cut blouse on and she was making sure her breast was recognize by others and it worked, I recognized them, not from personal experience just because every man like big breast or at least most man, little breast it good also, who am I kidding all breast is cool. I am sorry I am getting off track. She was short and had alright figure, but you can tell as she got older there was a good chance she might pick up weight and probably be overweight, so we walked in and she insisted I go to the counter first, so I walked up to the restaurant counter and place my order, then I went and set down at an empty table, it was a late lunch so maybe one other table in the restaurant was being occupied, she placed her order and came over and set at a table next to my table. I had some little business cards made that I carried with me and passed them out periodically for promotional purposes, my cards had a picture of the cover of my book along with my website, email address and my cell number. I asked her if she liked poetry, she said yes, I gave her one of my business cards, I asked her what's your name she said Lisa, I told her my name is Harry, she said you work around here, I told her I work at the CSD a few blocks up. The lady called me for my food order; my order was to go so I told Lisa bye, grabbed my food, she ask me if I wanted to eat my lunch there, I told her I had to get back to the office and work these cases, she said ok take care, I went to get in my car, I looked back at her she smile at me I got in my car and went back to work.

Approximately two weeks later I was at home over the weekend; doing my honey dues around the house, you know yard work take out the garbage, next thing I know my phone ring with a nine, one, six number popped up I did not answer because I do not answer numbers I do not recognize, I figure if it is that important they would leave a message, they did not leave a message. Later on in the evening I received another call from the same nine, one, six number no message left on my voice mail, about two hours later I receive another call this was on a Saturday night about eight PM I decided to answer the call, I said hello, a woman said hello, I said can I help you, she said Harry this is Kathy, I said Kathy who? She said you help me with my CS case in So-Low; I said girl! How did you get my number? You gave me one of your cards, I said no I did not! She said yes you did; I was the girl you met at the restaurant the other day. I said that girl told me her name is Lisa, she said yeah, I'm Lisa. I said are you fucking crazy? I said the father of your child told me you were crazy, I did not know he was talking this fucking crazy, I said what; you are stocking me now. You cannot be calling me outside my office, I said what the hell is wrong with you? I said I could get fired for this shit, she said I just want to talk and get to know you better, she said I always enjoy talking to you about my case, I just thought we could be friends outside of work. I said what type of friends you want to be. She said any type of friends you want to be; she was in her mid to later twenties and I was in my fifties. I said you are crazier than a motherfucker! I'm married and been married for years, I said I am not going to lay up with you, so you could get pregnant by my ass, not going to happen. I have this quote by a great philosopher who played a character in the Little Rascals; Matthew "Stymie" Beard, he said you might have choked Artie, but you are not going to choke Stymie! I always said, "You might choke Artie but you not going to choke Harry!" I could see myself laying up with this young lady who will tell you she is on birth control, and she have a baby by me; before I get off the pussy. I told her do not call me again, you know that girl continued calling me about ten times that evening. I wanted to whoop that bitch ass (excuse my language!) I was pissed off she was calling me at home, I was not answering the calls, she just continues to call my cell phone, I had to turn my cell phone down and off so my wife and kids don't hear it continually ringing, that bitch would not stop calling me, she must have called me approximated ten to twelve times through the night. I was thinking; I have a crazy ass bitch on my hands, I did not get much sleep through the night because I was trying to figure out how I was going to get out this situation that I did not have any intention of getting in too, I knew this girl was not mentally stable, I was thinking I had a fatal attraction, I was glad I did not have a rabbit or this bitch would have boiled it. Sunday she was calling me all day again wanting to talk to me about whatever, she did not care what we talked about, just as long as we were talking; I knew this woman for about eight months at this time. I answer one of the calls on Sunday; I said bitch stop calling me! I asked why you want to talk to me; she told me, I was like a father figure to her, and she enjoyed talking to me. I asked her do you fuck your father, she said no and started to laugh, she said I like how you looked at the restaurant and you have a good personality, I told her I do not care what you like, you must stop calling me all the time. I said you call me at work and work only; I do not think about those cases over the weekend, the weekends are for me and my family, I also told her do not be call me all day at work, I have more than just your case to handle; then I hung up the phone, she called back about twenty minutes later, I told myself; I'm going to kill that hoe! All my friends were calling me Captain Save A Hoe from the E-40 song; I use to laugh about it, now I was starting to believe it, because this woman is falling right into the hoe category in a hurry. I told myself I cannot wait to get to work tomorrow and call this bitch from work, she got to stop this shit, she continued to call and I did not answer, so she started texting me message and sending me pictures of her breast, I would be walk through my home and next thing l know my phone would vibrate and there would be some big ass titties looking at me, she would send me pictures of her other body parts also. I started thinking I need to let my supervisor know about this girl because she was going to get me fired if I do not report these incidences and I could not have that. You might have choked Artie, but you not going to choke Harry, when I got to work on Monday, I walked straight to my supervisor office which at the time was the lady that interviewed for fifteen minutes, started crying and then went home for the rest of week, came back to work on the following Monday and received the assistance supervisor position over me, because I did not layup with my former supervisor Pam. I told her all about Kathy constant phone calls but not about the pictures she was sending me; she said we just transferred her case to you so I must continue to work the case, she said I should not have given her my poetry card, I said I did not know who she was when I gave her the card. I told her to take her case out of my case load, she refuse, she said she thought I was best person to handle the case in the office, I said why; because I am black and the non-custodial and custodial parent was black, she said yes, she said she have faith in me handling the case, she also said and no one else wanted the case. Kathy name was known all over the office, I continued to work her case and she continues to send me her titties, all over my cell phone and drive me crazy with her insanity. She started talking about how she wishes I was her boyfriend; if we can get together and make love to each other, I told her I was married but that did not make a difference, she was talking about I had a good job, and she want a man in her life, not a boy like her baby's father Richard. I told her there are a lot of good man out there her age; she gave me that old saying "age is nothing but a number," I told her I do not want you Kathy, I told her just in the six to eight months I known her I would not want her as my girlfriend, wife or friend, she would talk about how pretty our baby would be, I would think to myself how crazy this bitch really is, I told myself this bitch will have me paying child support for the rest of my life if I laid up with her, so I said girl are you taking birth control just to ask, she said yes, I said was you taking birth control when you laid up with Richard, she said yeah, but she must have miss a day during that week. I thought to myself this is a dumb ass bitch;

if she thinks I will fall for that shit; I am not the type of person to call a woman out of her name, but some women need to be called a bitch, especially when she act like one on a daily basis.

I was just starting get her babies daddy to start making some type of payments; he was not paying the amount the courts order him to pay, but he was starting to make payments which gave me an opportunity to release his license so he can get a job, you cannot get a job without a valid driver license, and I cannot release his license without making some type of payment, there some occasion a person license can be released without some type of payment, when he find a job I will issue a wage assignment at the court order amount to his or her place of employment. Her babies daddy was mostly selling dope, he was saying he has too many kids to get a job, I was telling him we would take fifty percent of his disposable income, after taxes, he said he cannot live off that, I said but you will be paying the majority of your child support, after all he had six kids from five different women, his life was basically over, he said what if I get a second job, I told him we are going to take fifty percent of that money also, I told him he can pay, he can move to Iraq, or he can die, those are the only options he has to get out of paying CS. I told the young man this CS will literally kill you, it is not going anywhere but up in debt, I tried to explain to him in the simples terms so he can understand, he will need to take care of this matter, I did not want this young man to get in his forties and be four or five hundred thousand in the hold with CS debt and earning ten percent interest annually on top of that. Let me repeat myself so I can make sure you heard me correctly, four or five hundred thousand dollars in the hold and earning ten percent annually. He would work for a few more weeks and get fire or quit the job at a fast food restaurant or a warehouse job, his education was minimal at best, you have an uneducated young Black man trying to be a rapper and refusing to get a job or a trade, something

119

that would give he or she a good living but instead the young man or women born in poverty choose to fuck in the back seat of Cadillac, this is not making love, you have the perfect example of kids having kids this is one of the worse problems for our country. I am not saying this did not happen in other nationalities; but I hate seeing it in the African American race, because I knew from personal experience how difficult it was going to be for him and his family to survive, it is a difficult enough task for educated individuals all over the country to raise their family. Health and human services in every county across this country see kids having kids, this case is a perfect example of that scenario, young man and women having sex without protection and thinking the good feeling and secretion or nut, is fun, it can also make a child, then it turns from fun to responsibility. Responsibility is not as fun as the nut or the secretion which ever you choose to call it. I tried everything to talk some scene into this young man and stop him for ruining his life anymore then he already has; but he refuse to listen to a word I was telling him, so everything I told him proceeded to happening to him. He quit his job, his license got suspended again, I learned over my twenty years of employment with the CSD sometime you have to let a person run until he get tired, then he will quit running and get a job, but what he does not understand is his social security number is being run by the state and federal government twenty four-seven, once the state and feds received a bullseye on his social security number a wage assignment will be issued immediately even on a Sunday the document will be produced and faxed to his or her new place of employment. When it comes to CS it is cheaper to keeper her because it will bend a person over, male or female, whoever walk out the house, it will fuck the shit out of you literally and if Richard continues down the road he is on, he will find out every word I told him is true.

Now let's go back to Psycho, the mother, she continues to drive me nuts with calls every day. She wanted her money and she also wanted to talk to me, she was the first woman that pursued me to the point I was thinking about killer her ass or myself, this lady did not give a damn about no other woman's case, her case was the only case that matter. I refuse to spend all my time working her case and talking to her when I had thousands of parents depending on me to help them support their child or children. She insisted I work her case instead of other cases, I told her she was crazy and I was not going to give her more time then I give other custodial parents, I said a matter of fact now I have talk to you for too long and I hung up the phone on her ass, she was like a bad wife that nags the hell out of someone, you know nag, nag, nag, nag nag! I continue to work other cases; she continued to call me and leave messages I still would receive up to fifteen message within an eight hour period per day, she was calling me on work phone and my cell phone, I would receive ten messages on my cell and fifteen messages on my work phone, I would let my supervisor listen to the messages and she would say you have a real fan; she left her case in my case load because she was black woman, none of my co-workers wanted to deal with an African American male or female, and especially this Black woman. As many times l walked around the office and I turned down a hallway and one of the man or women walking toward me would say "Oh Harry, you scared me, or you startled me" I heard that at least once a month during my twenty years of employment.

I continued to work Psycho case to the best of my ability, I remember the holiday season was coming up, Kathy started crying every time I spoke to her, she was talking about her son wanted a Play Station two or three, she was talking about how she is trying save up three hundred dollars to buy one for him, she tried to contact his father Richard but he was refusing to give her anything and she would call and when I answered her call she would be crying her eyes out every time we talked

121

about how her kids is only going to get one present for Christmas and it is not going to be the present he wanted because she has to pay her rent and all the other bills by herself, she not going to be able to afford to buy him the Play Station Unit he wanted. During the month of December she continued to call me and cry on the phone on my voice mail messages she would say; I called Richard and he is refusing to give me any money to help his son, I say to myself dam now this bitch is crying every time I talk to her, she did not know that was a weakness of mine, I hate when a woman start crying, I did not like seeing my mother crying while I was a young child. My mother did not cry a lot but when she cried it always made me feel really bad, I seen her cry when John F. Kennedy was shot and killed, when the Rev. Martin Luther King Jr. was shot and killed and when Robert F. Kennedy was shot and killed I would do almost anything to stop a woman from crying as long as I was not real mad at her for some reason. I would not answer her calls sometime because I knew she was going to be crying and I did not want to hear that shit. She continued to call, and I made the mistake of answering the phone at about a quarter to five in the evening, I got off work at five, that bitch kept me on the phone until about five thirty in the evening crying! I started thinking this bitch has been crying for the last forty minutes about a damn Play Station Unit; she had finally worn me down, I told that bitch that I would loan her one hundred dollars toward the Play Station if she would just shut the fuck up and quit crying, I could not take talking to her any longer and listen to her crying, I was thinking my kids was getting everything they needed and wanted, my wife and I was doing alright financially, we can afford the hundred dollars and it is Christmas time. I took the money from what I like to call my stash on the side; she said so you are going to buy the Play Station? I said hell no! Play Station was costing approximately three hundred dollars for the unit at this time, I will loan you one hundred dollars toward the unit, I am not buying shit, she said you going to bring the hundred dollars to me, we can meet for dinner, I said hell no! I am not going to meet you for dinner, what you are going to pay for dinner out of the hundred that I loaning you? She said how I am I going to get the money, I asked her what bank she bank with? She said Silverton Credit Union, I told her to text me her bank account number and I will deposit the money in her account, I said now get your ass off my line, I will put the money in your account next week, I hung up the phone on that bitch! So, I guess my repayment for my generosity was pictures of her breasts and other body parts down low started coming in over the weekend on my cell phone. I guess that is the reason all my friends called me Captain Save-A-Hoe! I hated that bitch because she was jumping up and down on my nerves and making my job more difficult to complete, but I still was not going to let the young Black child suffer because he was born to two idiots; two people that was not mature enough to accept responsibility to raise a child. I guess you could blame my good heart during the Christmas season or maybe deep down inside I was really Captain Save-A-Hoe. About the pictures, do not get me wrong, I looked at the pictures and I said damn to myself a couple of times, then I saved the pictures to my phone just in case I would need these pictures at a later date. I looked at the pictures because I am a man; I saved them in case I had to protect my ass, my mother taught me to always protect my own ass first then help someone else. I guess that is why on the airplanes the flight attendants tell you to put your oxygen mask on before you put on your child's mask, you have to protect your ass first, before you can protect someone else's ass. She made sure she sent me her account number, I made the deposit into her account the following week, and then she proceeds to ask me if I can deposit a hundred dollars in her account per month to help her out. I just hung up the phone on that crazy ass bitch! I handled her case for about two years total; it was in or around my eighteenth year of employment at So-low at this time. She told me her parents was going to help her get his Play Station for him I told her good, after Christmas and New Years passed. A new year rolled in; I am still working my cases and trying to bring money in for the children in my caseload, she still trying to interrupt my days but I did not have problem sending her straight to voice mail, she got mad and came into the office wanting to talk to me directly, I came down stairs, she was asking me why I was not answering her calls, I told her I have already explained why I am not accepting her calls all the time, I said I told you to stop calling me every day, let along every fifteen minutes of my day. I told her she is going to lose her job because she is calling me; I told her to go home and quit calling me all the time, I told her do not call me, I will call you. I did not take another call from her for about a week, yes, she was still calling me on my private line over the weekend, but I did not answer my line. One day she called my office and I made the mistake of answering my phone; we started talking she sound depressed she started saying why she cannot find someone like me, I said girl you do not even know me, then she said sometime I think about killing myself, I would think to myself go ahead, then I started thinking should I send a police officer by her apartment, suicide came up a couple times during our conversation I told her then who would take care of her son, he need you in his life, then she switched to another conversation and said she has an address for Richard, I said this is about the sixth address you gave us for Richard the last five address has been wrong, I said didn't you tell me you work for the state, I said where are you getting all these addresses from? She just flew off the handle; and said what you trying to get me fired, then she said if you are going to try to get me fired, then I am going to get you fired! I started to laugh, and then I say why do I want to get you fired? I said I am trying to get money for you, why do

I want to get you fire? She said you are trying to say I am using the states system to located Richard, I said I am not saying anything, all I ask you was where are you getting your information from, you flew off the handle and started insinuating I believe you are getting your info off the state system. I told her the system we have in our office is just as good or better, I told her to let me handle the search, she said you are trying to get me fired. I said why do I want to get you fired; you knucklehead, she hung up her phone, I said good maybe she will quit calling me all the time. About a week later I get called to my Director's office she said I had a formal complaint filed against me from a custodial parent a woman name Kathy; she stated I was going to call her supervisor and try to get her terminated from her job, I told Rhonda she was the woman who I have already brought to every bodies attention in this office, I spoke to my supervisor Carol and several of my co-workers, supervisors, attorney's and even you Rhonda. She told me I had to go to the main administration office and have a mediation with an independent mediator, she said independent mediator was going to meet with Kathy and then meet with me. When the mediator called me to schedule my deposition; I told him we do not even have to wait until next schedule date to take care of this situation, I told him we can take care of this right now, he said no let's wait until next week. The following week came up, I called my union representative up and had him meet me at the mediation just to witness the deposition, the mediator was already videotaping and recording the deposition, we all had our recorders out, I had my little Sony Digital Recorder I carried in my bag, my co-workers called the bag my purse, it was a cloth bag that had two handles made out of the same material, like a book bag, or my man purse. The mediator Mr. Harris was a white gentleman who was asking me questions, as I explained the situation, he found some lies in her story and it came clear she was full of shit. He asks me did I call her supervisor to try to get her fired. I said no, if I called her supervisor and got her fired, then the kid has two unemployed parents in his life, I said that would not have done me any good, I am not in the business of getting people fired, I'm in the business of getting people money for the custodial parents so she or he can support their children and helping non-custodial parents get hired so they can pay their child support, I told him she came to that conclusion on her own, I never told her I was going to call her management, never mention it, Mr. Harris said, she said I asked her to meet her for dinner, I told him she crazier than I thought she was, after he heard the entire story he knew she was lien and no good. I told him about her stocking me and calling me at home, I never told him about the photos she was sending me and the money I loaned her, she is sending me her address asking me to come visit her I was keeping all that in my back pocket just in case I needed it at a later date. I did not know what So-Low was going to do; I know one thing So-Low was not going to have my back, I know that for fact, I was planning to pull all the photos and texts out when we were in court. All my co-workers was distancing themselves from me after I received the complaint, that's from the director on down to my co-workers, the only person that was really talking to me was our janitor Joe, this old white man and former recovering alcoholic, drug addict that came in after five PM to clean, empty garbage cans and vacuum the office, he ended up getting moved to another location because one of my co-workers did not like the way he was looking at them, I thought to myself, one of the women must have been walking around in their short skirt or low cut blouse and Joe must have took a peek and they got upset, I found out later on it was a male co-worker name Stew who said he looked at him in the wrong way, I was cracking up when I found out, I always thought Stew had a little sugar in his tank, I thought Stew had more vegetable then meat in his stew, not that anything is wrong with that. Back to all my co-workers they were running from me like I had the plague, when I came out clean everyone was saying they are so happy everything worked out for me. I always thought to myself they do not give a damn about me; these are my five a day week friends, they were causing me unnecessary headaches with their bullshit, I had gone through in the past, maybe one or two of them really had my wellbeing at heart. After the mediation Mr. Harris decided in my favor and dismissed my case; he stated he was going to contact Kathy and tell her not to contact me any longer, he recommended taking her case out of my case load, I immediately had Carol take Kathy's case out of my caseload, it was no way I was going to help her from that point on, even if Carol would have not have taken the case away from me, she still did not technically have to take the case, if she chose not too. Kathy called me a couple times, and I told that bitch to get her ass off my line and I told her never to call me again, she said she was sorry, she tried calling me on my cell phone and I called her all types a bitches and hoe's, she hung up on me this time, she miss me working her account, I worked back end collection, meaning the people that was not paying and did not want to pay, that was the reason her case was transferred to me, I was position there for a reason, I had a strong legal collection background, collectors did not want to work the cases I was working and bring in money. I was dealing with the most harden parents; the ones who did not like how the kid was conceived rather by accident, misled, cheating, side piece, girlfriend, wife, lies or just plain did not want the child, you take your pick how your little boy or girl got here, the fact of the matter is they are here and if your dick was in his or her mother's vagina, your semen reach her mother's egg, the baby percolates for nine months and see the lights of the delivery room! The courts do not take a man's word any longer; the courts will give you a choice to take a DNA test at the cost of the state, if you say no then you are the father if you take the test and the test come back stating you are the father, then you are that baby's daddy! No if ands or buts! You are obligated to raise the child or children to the age of eighteen or until the child graduate high school, some states you have to raise the child to the age of twenty-one, some states if the child is in an accredited college you will be obligated to pay for the child. Back to Kathy she finally got the message and stopped harassing me, I started considering retirement after I had to handle her case, plus I was going into approximately my eighteen years of employment, I started thinking about it a little more often. I started to think society did not appreciate what I was doing and when you are not appreciated in your home office that could also make a man's mind wonder. I never did get my money from that bitch, but it was worth a hundred to get rid of her ass, worth every penny. That is the way I looked at it, she will need me, before I need her; she jeopardized my life and my family life, which is a no, no with me! Her stupidity could have affected my life and I was sincerely trying to help her, you never know what is going on in someone else head, like this old man use to say, "One of her chairs have turned over", he would say this when someone would do something or say something crazy! Her actions could have been disastrous for me and my family, here I am doing everything I can do to keep my family healthy and a float, and some idiots come alone and try to ruin everything you work for the last twenty years of your life, I could never respect anyone who does something like this purposely. I would like to quote the great philosopher Della Reese in the movie Harlem Nights and tell her she can kiss my entire ass! Good riddance, Arrivederci, Adios, Good bye, Tata and get your Stanking Ass out of here! That is just me! Next up with Craziness.

COURTS

The court system is another process you will have to deal with if you or your worst or better half cannot come to an amicable solution. If the two parties are able to come to an amicable solution, then the court is not needed other than to draw up the legal agreement documents between the parents. If there are verbal abuse, physical abuse, child abuse involved than the courts will come into the game and start officiating your relationship because obviously the two individuals involved cannot agree on time with your child, how much financial support the non-custodial parent is to pay each month, what other activities each parent has to cover for example your child's sporting events, music lessons, and other activities, who will be paying child care for the children, and who will be claiming the child or children on their taxes, issues like these would have to be hashed out. There is all these issues that must be answered and more before the case is complete. The state has a formula and a form that you can complete online, you can run a calculation and come up with the support amount that the non-custodial parent will have to pay, the calculation may not be the exact amount therefore every county has an in-house counsel that would assist you for no charge. This counsel is called the Family Law Facilitator or one of the in-house attorneys for the CSD will review your application and have all parties sign documents including all attorney's involved, rather personal attorney or not. The documents are filed with the courts and from this point on all agreements are permanent and binding until the parties go to court again to change the agreement. A judge must sign off on all modifications from that point on, even if the mother and father come to a different agreement it must be signed off by the courts.

I remember one particular incident in court room. This father came into the CSD, he had three kids with him two from his first wife, and one child with his second wife who came to the division with him this particular day. He wanted to get full custody of his two children with his first wife; he said she is having mental issue from heavy drug use, and he does not believe his two young boys approximately six and seven years old are safe when they spend a weekend with their mother. The father said the boys come home with bruises they should not have every weekend they stay with their mother; one of his sons had been burned by a cigarette, he called his boys over to the interviewing booth and asked them if they like going and staying with their mother for the weekends, they both said no, he say they cry every time they have to go stay with their mother. He told me when she get mad she will start punching herself in the face, I said she will start punching her own self in the face, he said yes, she will punch herself in the face, I looked at his second wife sitting there and asked her if she witness this action by his first wife, his wife said yes she seen her punch herself. I spoke to our attorney and we agreed to get this case on the court calendar so we can get this custody and visitation issues straighten out, we do not want her to hurt those boys. I had the mother served; she came into the office and want to talk to me before her court date, she was a nice looking white young lady who looked like she did not have any issues, she was a little hot headed but for the most part she handled herself well. I told her to make sure she show for court and the judge will have to make the decision on her visitation. She must have used drugs and alcohol the prior night because she was looking all sluggish when she arrive to court, the judge made the determination he will order supervised visitation the father agreed, supervised visitation is a two hour visitation with a mutual agreed adult watching the enter action between the child and his mother it usually take place at a park and the mother in this case has to pay one hundred dollars for the time. The mother was pissed and all of a sudden she started punching herself in the face repeatedly; to the point her mouth started bleeding, eye swelling and she was crying profusely in court to the point the bailiff had to come over and escort her out of the building, we found out that she was diagnosis as a manic depressed young lady and was also an paranoid schizophrenic, she needed supervised visitation with her children, the father was Mexican and he said he knew something was wrong with her, he was happy I was able to help him. Next!

MR. ADOPTION

For the last ten years or more of my employment with So-Low I represented them in court. I have helped a variety of people that came into court with all types of different issues. One time this young man met this woman that had four kids by three different men, they walked into our office and our receptionist called me, the man asked me if they can talk to me in private, so I took the man and woman into this private room that we had available the women looked a little older then the young man she looked in her mid-thirties and he looked in his mid to early twenties. I said how can I help you? He looked at me and he told me he want to adopt all four of her kids, I said these are not your kids? They said no, I said none of them? They said no, I asked the woman to step out of the room I will need to talk to the young man alone. She and the kids stepped out of the room and I asked the young man how old are you? He said I am twenty-four years old, I asked the young man, are you crazy? He said no, I'm not crazy, I thought to myself no you must be pussy whooped, he said he love this woman and her kids, I asked how long had they been together? He said they been together for about eight months, I asked him where is the three father's living he said two of the fathers are living in another state and the other father of the twins is in state prison and will be there for at least another ten to fifteen years. He stated she cannot locate the two fathers that lives out of state. I said to him none of these children are your obligation, he said he knows, I said have you mention this to his parents, he said they would not care, I told him that will make then their grandkids, don't you think they might want to know they are getting four grandkids overnight. I told him I would want to know, I told him I want you to understand that if he is able to adopt these kids and if they separate for any reason he will be held responsible for these kids until all four children reached the age of eighteen and graduate high school. He said he is ready for the challenge, I have good jobs, I said where are you working? He told me he had two jobs he worked at a tire shop and at a restaurant. I told him if I was him I would not adopt those kids, but if you want too, it is your decision that you and the mother has to make, I also told him the fathers have to agree to adoption when we locate them, I said the one in prison might agree to the adoption but we have to find out what the other two fathers have to say. I invited the mother back in the room and her four kids and went over all the necessary steps that was needed for him to adopt the children, I gave them all the necessary documents to complete his task and let them know the fathers will have to agree to the adoptions.

He was able to adopt the four kids, and they got married. They was living together for about four years before the mother walked in our office and was talking about she is going through a divorce, and she wanted to open up a child support case against the father of her five children. I did not recognize her when she came into the office, but when they appeared in court to discuss the child support I looked at him and I said to myself that is Mr. Adoption, he could not look me in my eyes, I was looking at him like you idiot, I told your dumb ass not to adopt those kids, and he done something else even more stupid, he had another kid, now he has five kids he is responsible for and four of the kids is not his biological kids by the time he left court he was in tears, literally. He had his mother with him, he had moved back home with his parents and we just took fifty percent of his disposable income from both his jobs and he still was not covering his entire child support amount. He had to start looking for another job to add to the two he got, or a better higher paying job, he also did not understand the more your income is the more he is going to have to pay. All the mother has to do is asked for a modification and the courts will recalculate and reevaluate her case to see if the non-custodial parent can pay more and do not let the children have piano lessons or playing sports. That young man has a good ass whooping coming, so let's move on to another incident.

SIXTEEN YEARS AND COUNTING!

One time I had this pretty white woman walk into the CSD and ask for help, she need to talk to an officer about opening up a case. The receptionist called me and asked me to help her, so I came down stairs to the interviewing booths I signed into the system in the booth and called her to the booth she came over and set down, she was a very pretty blond headed woman I said can I help you? She said she is a single mother with a sixteen year old son. She was using drug and alcohol pretty heavy back when he was conceived, she was never sure who the father maybe because she had a boyfriend but she was also messing around with more than just her boyfriend. When she became pregnant she was living in a fog from the alcohol and drug use, she stated she was use marijuana, cocaine, meth and alcohol she knew she had been involved with more than one man and she was not even sure who she was with and when she was with them. She thought about aborting the child but she really did not want to do that deep down inside so she chose to have the kid and try to raise the child on her own, she cleaned up her act and had her son. DNA testing was new when her son was born sixteen years ago it was a lot more advance when she entered my office. She stated her son has been asking her about his father while he was growing up and she had to tell him that she was not sure who his father was because she was using drugs and alcohol back then. She would started crying every time her son asked about his father she started crying in the booth I told her to stop crying we will try our best to locate your son's father. She said the reason she came in today while her son was at school was because she was at the supermarket the other day and ran into an old girlfriend that she use to hang out with back in those partying days and she said the woman asked if she married her old boyfriend name Ricky she was not sure if the child was Ricky's because he was the person she was fucking around on. I told her Ricky is where I am going to start my search, I asked if she knew where Ricky was living now, she said my old friend at the supermarket told her she heard he was living up north near Reno area. I asked her for Ricky's last name, she said Davis, she said he is a white gentleman about six feet tall, I asked when was the last time she spoke to him, she said it was when they had their last argument sixteen years ago. I told her I will search his name and get him in the office to have a DNA test. I had her bring her son a couple days later and I did a DNA test on her and her son, I search Ricky Davis in California and came up with a lot of them in California but only ten of them living in towns north of Sacramento. I started calling them one by one and asked them if they knew the custodial parent. I was down to the last three Ricky Davis and call the next numbers I spoke to a man, he asked me to call him at another number I called him at the other number it was his office, he said he ask me to call him at this number because he did not want his employee's to see him on his cell phone during business, I told him I understand. I ask Ricky if he ever heard of the custodial parent, he said yes, she was an old girlfriend of his, why? I asked him was they together about fifteen years ago, he said somewhere around there, Why? I told him she has a son that is sixteen and she was not sure who the father was and she stated you might be his dad, and we need him to go to a clinic in his area to take a DNA test. He exploded, he said she have never said anything to him about she was pregnant, he said I have another family, he stated he is married and have two kids now, he said this is going to cause him to get a divorce. I told him he does not have to tell his wife about this until he is sure the child is his kid, I told him I will have a packet mailed to him and he can complete the packet and take it to the lab where the DNA test will be completed. I asked for his address, he gave me his home address but he wanted the packet to be mailed to his place of business, he was a manager at a sporting goods store in a small town up north. I told him I will call him tomorrow and let him know what lab I would have him go to for the test. Ricky wanted to know will he have to pay sixteen years of back CS, I told him no, he will just have to pay for the next couple years, he was all shook up when we got off the phone, I called the mother and told her I found the possible father and she was happy I explained the process to her and she said she will wait until I get back to her and we will go from there. I called Ricky back the following day with his appointment information, I told him to make sure he have the documents completed, I explained the process and told him that we are just going to buckle swab the inside of his mouth and get some saliva and the lab will get back to CSD in a few days, I told him I will call him with the results, Ricky was sweating bullets waiting for the results a few days went by and we received the results, I opened up the lab envelope and pulled out the results I called Ricky he was nervous as can be on the other end of the phone. He said what is the results? I told him he is not the father but the percentage was close to his DNA but not close enough that I could name him the father. Ricky said thank God! He was not the father then Ricky said you said that the DNA percentage was close to it being my baby, he said my brother told him the night they broke up, my girlfriend walked into same bar he was in that night and he told him he fucked her that night. He and Ricky had stopped talking because of him fucking his girlfriend. I asked Ricky what is his brother's name he told me Robert, I said what is Robert's number Ricky gave me his number, I told Ricky not to let Robert know I will be calling him, he said we do not talk anyways. I knew Robert was most likely the child's father because the DNA result was so close to Ricky DNA that it had to be a relative. Ricky's results was like 94.3, I called the custodial parent and told her

137

Ricky was not the father of her child, I then asked her did she have sex with his older brother, she was ashamed to say she did have sex with him. I called Robert his brother and told him we will need to get him in for a DNA test because he maybe the father of her child he wanted to run, but he had a good job and could not run that far, I set Roberts appointment and had him go in to complete DNA test the results came back at 99.9 percentage, he was the father, we got him in court and he had to take care of this child for the next couple of years. The custodial parent was so happy for her son because she never felt good not knowing who his father was, and she was so grateful to me for locating her son's biological father. She did not want to be just pointing out men that she had laid up with when she was not sure who the father was she was doing a lot of partying at that time. Robert had his own family but was willing to build a relationship with his son. That shows you how life works the mother walked in a supermarket and ran into an old friend and their conversation triggered everything that lead her to the father of her child. She said she never thought this day would come, and good thing that child was under the age of eighteen because Robert would not have been obligated to take the test if the child was considered an adult. Robert would have the option to take the test, he could have also refused. The custodial parent received CS payment for the next couple of years and the young man got to know his father. I guess that is why my buddies was calling me Captain Save A Hoe!

NOT COOL!

This next experience is a about a Hispanic family that live in the town, they did not live together because the mother and father had separated after their three daughters was born, they was still married and had daughters age eight, ten, and twelve the custodial parent was the mother she had the kids the majority of the time. The father would come by on the weekends and stay the night when he was not drinking, he had a good job he was a manager for a good size trucking company but he was a mean drunk. One Friday night he came by late night after drinking and the mother refuse to let him in the home. He started yelling calling her bitches and whores outside the door and then he broke down the front door and proceeded to beat his wife and rape her while the three girls was watching and crying; as their mother was being sexually abused on the living room floor the mother did not resist after a while because she wanted to end the abuse as soon as possible, as you could imagine this was not the first time this happen, when he got done with her and she was able to get up, her eyes was black and her mouth had a bloody bottom lip and it swollen. He left the home knowing deep down inside he should have not done that to the woman he was suppose too love, he also knew that it was a good chance that he was going to have the police looking for him, the mother did call the police on him, and told them where they can locate him, he was picked up that night he woke up in the county jail the next morning.

The next week the mother walked in to the CSD and the receptionist called me she stated she has someone that she want me to talk too, I said ok, I will be down, I went down and call the young ladies name and she walked up with her three girls she had sunglasses on but it was an overcast day, when she sat down she stated she want to open a case, I could see some discoloration and swelling on her face, she was a very pretty women prior to her being beat up, I asked her what happen she told me about the above altercation and I told her that is good that motherfucker is in jail. I personally do not believe in a man beating a woman because any man that beats a woman is less than man to me. I grew up in a household where spousal abuse took place, not a lot but enough for me not to like it. She wanted to open up her case, she stated they had decided to leave the CSD out of their business when they separated so they made an agreement between the two parties she told him as long as he make his payments on time she would not ask CSD to get involved. Well after this last altercation she wanted us involved and we was more than happy to get involved. While I was assisting the Hispanic mother a co-worker of mine by the name of Maria walked behind my booth and saw the Hispanic mother sitting there and she noticed the woman's bruised face and her crying. Maria worked in the case opening department of the division and after I had the mother complete all the necessary documents to open her case, Maria came over to my office and I explained to her what happen to the young lady I was assisting, she told me to make sure she get to open that case, I said okay, I will bring you the file after I write it up and she will complete the intake portion of the case then I will get the file back and I will do the enforcement part of the case. Maria said she is married to a Mexican man? I told her yeah, she said Mexican man always beat their women, she had two children with a Mexican man and two kids with a White man who she was living with at this time, she said her first husband was Mexican he was the father of her first two kids, he hit her a couple time and the second time was the last time, she left his ass. Maria took her case and got that mother a four thousand dollar a month judgement for CS. Maria, our attorney and I was in court when he had to appear in front of the judge and the judgement was approved, the father had post bail while he was being held for the criminal charges and restraining order. I will never forget when the father called me crying stating there is no way he can afford to pay this amount his check was getting hit for fifty percent of his disposable income and he was still not covering the entire month payment. I spoke to Maria she said Harry, fuck him; you see how bad he beat her, I said yeah! She said do not give him a modification for at least six months, I told her ok, we was cracking up, you can ask for a modification once a year this was his first year so he had to wait until the following year before he can get a modification that means he was stuck paying the judgement amount for at least a year. The mother called me and said she received an auto deposit for almost two thousand dollars. I asked her how much was their agreement prior to the CSD running our numbers she said seven hundred dollars a month, I told her there is a new sheriff in town, the next day she came in the office because she wanted to hug me she was crying because of how much assistance we gave her, I told her Maria also helped on her case she told me to make sure I told her thank you. I told Maria the custodial parent said thanks, I told the father he better think twice about putting his hands on his wife next time because he was not using his head and now that the CSD is involved I explained everything that could happen to him now that we are involved, like license suspension, bank levies, wage assignments, passport shut down just to name a few. He slapped his wife upside her head and we slapped that motherfucker upside his head some time hitting your pocket book hurts more than a physical slap upside your head. I guess that is why my buddies was calling me Captain Save a Hoe!

BRAVE YOUNG LADY AND HER LITTLE BROTHER

This next experience is about a brave young lady that stood up for herself and her little brother when no one else would, but me! One day I got called by our receptionist to help a lady with her child support case. I went down to the first floor and met with the custodial parent she had a fifteen year old daughter and a seven year old boy with her, she wanted to know if she could get a modification because she seen her ex-husband driving a new car and she thought he was making more money, she wanted more money out of him that is how relationships are, depending on the woman or man you end up with rather married or not. While I was assisting their mother with her case I would occasionally glance up and look at her daughter and smile at her she would semi smile back, her little brother would just keep his head down and continued to look at the floor her daughter would look at me sometimes like she want to tell me something, I asked her was she alright and she would said yes in a very quiet manner. I glance at her again periodically and something was tell me she had some type of issue she was dealing with and she did not want her mother to know about it. She was a pretty little white girl and her little brother was sitting there like he was afraid to talk or say anything, I notice he would never look up from the floor and he would not say anything not even hi. Their mother and I completed our business and I collected the modification application and told her I would get back to her once we started work on her case. While they was walking out of the office the little girl eyes glance back like they was screaming for help but I did not know what her eyes was saying.

The next day I got another call from the receptionist this time she tell me she had a fifteen year old girl and her little brother in the office asking if they can talk to me, my receptionist tell me she believe it is the same two children that walked in and talk to me yesterday with their mother. I came down to the first floor where we have our interviewing booths, the young lady come to the booth with her little brother and she asked me if I remember them, I said you came in the office with your mother yesterday, she yes, that was us, I asked why are you two back to talk to me without your mother, I told them they are minors and I should not be talking to them without their parents present, the young lady started to cry, I told her don't cry as I gave her a tissue, I said what is wrong? She stated her mother's got a new boyfriend after her mother and their father separated and he has been molesting her and her little brother. I said what do you mean molesting you? She stated he had sexual intercourse with her, I asked how old are you, she said fifteen, she said she have never had sex before, I said how long has this been going on? She stated about eight months, I looked at her little brother and he kept his head down, I told her little brother to look up it was hard for him to do, when he finally looked up, I asked him has his mother's boyfriend been hurting him, he just looked down at the floor again, I asked him again was his mother's boyfriend hurting him in anyway, and he said yes real quietly, I said have he been touching his private parts, he said yes real low and started to cry, I asked have they told their mother and they both said yes, but she does not believe them. They said their mother goes to work every day and she leave them with him during her work hours. They said almost every day he have sex with one of them and then he threaten to hurt them if they say anything to their mother. The young lady said her brother had a small parakeet bird in a cage in his room, and her mother's boyfriend gabbed the bird and told the little boy if he tell his mother he would do this to him and he squeezed the little bird in his hand until the bird's guts came out of his mouth, then he went to the local pets store and purchased another bird before their mother return from work. They was both afraid of what her boyfriend would do if they continue to stay in the home, I told her he has already done way too much. The young lady said she told her brother to walk down to the office where her mother went yesterday and let's talk to that black man their mother spoke too, maybe he can help us. I asked if they told their father and they said their mother always be listening to their phone calls with their father. I told them to sit tight while I make a couple phone, I told them I have to make the calls from my office. I went back upstairs to my office and I called CPS and spoke to this lady I knew that was working in that department, I told her I have a couple kids I believe she will need to talk too today! I told her of their situation so she said she will come down to my office and pick the kids up and bring them back to her office, I told her I will notate my case in the CSD that I call her and what the children told me. I went back down to the first floor told the kids they are going to be alright. I asked if they had someone else they can stay with and they said their father or an aunt, I told them a lady from CPS will be picking them up and they want them to have an complete medical examination on them both, It turned out that her mother's boyfriend had took the girl virginity and had penetrated the young boys rectum to the point that he was going to need surgery to repair the damage. They arrested the mother and her boyfriend that day, this was a terrible day for me after they came into the office. Some time you hear things and your day and life will never be the same, this was one of those days. This day made me sick to my stomach it took a while before I was able to stomach it. Both the mother and her boyfriend had to do time in prison the mother received a year and had to completing parenting classes, her boyfriend received a ten year prison stretch and have to register as a sex offender for the rest of his life. I help the father and their aunt get temporary custody of his two children, they was real grateful for what I did for them, both kids hug me even though the boy was hesitant and I do not blame him, but we all assured him that he is safe now. I gave both of them my business card told them to call me if they ever need me again. You would be surprised how often this scenario happens the mother and father separated and the mother gets another boyfriend and the boyfriend moves in to the home and molest the children and when the children tell their mother, the mother refuse to believe them. Next time your child or children tell you something believe them until you have good reason not to believe them. Do not just ignore what they are saying because most of the time they are being honest and also be aware of their behavior because it will also change. A child will become subdue or start acting out to the point that you will not be able to recognize he or she, he or she will become an entirely different person, their smile will leave and turn into a frown on their face, do not talk as much, there is a lot of signs, I am not a expert child psychologist, I seen enough video and done enough surveys alone with my experience to tell you it is up to you to keep the lines of communication open you should let your child know he or she can talk to you about anything at any time. It is a must situation that you do, it could mean life death or prison time you never know. Next!

WHAT! NO, NO, NO! OK!

This next experience is something that happen at least ten times or more to me during my twenty year work history at So-Low CSD. During my years at the division there was a mini movement started after a woman was in a restaurant or park and they pulled their breast out to feed their babies. They was asked to put their titties away while people was eating and walking through the park. Breast feeding in public hit the scene and when the news got a hold of it, it went nationwide and next thing you know every woman walking in the CSD was pulling their titties out on a regular bases. It did not bother me personally I rather enjoyed it, I did not have anything against it, I was all for it, if a woman was comfortable enough to breast feed, then more power to her, the baby is hungry and the mother is the main avenue to feeding the child at that time, then what is the problem. One time a white lady came into the office and I was called down to help her she was a nice looking lady approaching the beginning stage of becoming heavy set, she was in the office checking on her support, it was running a little later and she wanted an update, she lived in the apartment complex not far from our office so she would walk down to the office with her infant and her son, I seen her before and had talk to her on the phone on more than one occasion. Her two kids with her is a four year old boy and an infant in a removable car seat chair. While I was bring up the computer in the interviewing booth she reached down and pull the baby out of the chair on the floor, then she reached in her blouse and pulled her right titty out, this was a big ass titty it came down and landed on the counter, her nipple was looking at me like a dead fish with one eye, I looked back at it because I thought it was looking at me, then she grabbed the big ass titty and started positioning it in the infants mouth, so I tried my best not to continue looking at her titty and started discussing her case. As I was discussing her case I see the four year boy stop playing with the toys we had in our lobby to entertain the kids and start walking toward the booth when he got to the booth he start to reaching for the mother's left titty and the mother say son you want some while he has one hand resting on her left titty, her son climbed on to her lap, I am thinking to myself please do not pull your left titty out, please do not pull your left titty out, please do not pull your left titty out, she sat the baby on the counter and reached in her blouse and pulled out her big ass left titty and plopped it down on the counter, good thing the left titty did not hit the four year old boy on the head because it would have put a knot on his head or at least shook him up mentally, he would have to go in NFL concussion protocol, the left titty was laying there looking at me like the one eyed cyclops, my mouth started to water and I was looking at it with my mouth open trying not to get aroused, because I am a man and a man who like titties! I apologize if I offended anyone, but I am not going to apologize for liking titties, back to the incident the four year old boy grab the big ass left titty and put it in his mouth and started sucking on the left titty while looking up at me smiling and showing me the titty, while saying no more titties for you, his mother was telling him to stop saying that to Mr. Johnson, I wanted to whoop his ass, I was looking at him like you too dam old to still be nursing on some titties, so I continue to help the mother while both of her titties are all over my counter, I did not have enough room on my counter for my paper work, a female co-worker walked behind my booth while the titty smorgasbord was going on. She was cracking up, because she seen me trying to be professional while those two big ass titties was looking at me. I wish I had a drink and a cigarette while those titties was sitting in front of me, I finally got her and her kids taken care of

147

and out of the office. I had to sit in the booth until my body part went back to normal then I went back up to my office. I started thinking the mother must have enjoyed them babies sucking on her titties at the same time, she must have received some type of pleasurable sensation out of breastfeeding the infant and the four year old grown man. This happen to me many of time during my work history, I am going to be honest I enjoy every titty that was pulled out in front me, some of the women was fine and some of them not so fine every time a mother pulled her titty out, I tried my best not to look at the titty but I could not do it, no matter how hard I tried, I could not do it and for that I am sorry! Some of those mothers knew exactly what they was doing. I use to say titties are the only two suckers in this world I trusted, some of my co-worker would crack-up. Let's me quit while I am behind and move away from the titty section of my book.

SIXTEEN AND COUNTING!

This next experience is about a Black non-custodial parent a man that live in the Bay Area which was approximately two hours south of my employment. He walked in our office and our receptionist called me down, I took the elevator down to the first floor and met with the gentleman he was about six two dark skin Black man with a well-groomed full beard, I do not judge men but he had the Theodore Pendergrass look tall and slender he looked like a lot of women like him. I said how can I help you? He said I need help with my CS, I pulled this brother cases up on the booth computer and he had sixteen cases with sixteen different women, I looked at him and said damn are you in the Guinness Book of World Records! I had to keep counting over and over again to make sure I was looking at the system correctly, I said you have sixteen total cases, he said yeah, I have sixteen kids, he had kids in every area code I said do you know all of them, he said yes, he said he also knows where every kids lived and could reach them if he need too and their mother's. I said every woman you laid up with had a baby by you, he said almost, he had babies in the Bay Area, Los Angeles, Nevada, New York and New Orleans just to name a few and he did not have any money, he basically did not work, he said it is not worth him working he was selling drugs because he had so many kids, he had eight boys and eight girls, I told him after we got comfortable with each other because I had plenty of time to get comfortable with him because I reviewed all sixteen cases with him and gave him an update on each case, I told him he need to name the next two kids Get Off and Stay Off, we laughed and I talked him in to making a payment on his cases of three hundred dollars so I can get his license released, it was not going to stay released unless he was able to continued making payments every month, which he was not, the payments prior to the three hundred dollars that day was about two years earlier I just wanted to get some money out of him, the three hundred dollars would have been split between the kids who was not on welfare at the time. So if there was a mother that was not on welfare she would receive the entire three hundred because the other mothers are receiving some type of assistance from the states and plus the states will give mothers that is on aid a fifty dollar check per month so they can buy their alcohol and cigarettes each month it is called a disregard payment all the rest of her money will be on the EBT card which the states replaced for food stamps. The majority of his mother's was all on aid the mothers was all different nationality, he told me which mother's he liked and the ones he did not like, he had Asians, about three White women and about four Black women and a few Mexican women I cannot remember the exact break down, he said he love every one of his kids and he make sure he see them when he can or when the mothers allow him to see them he send them money when he has it, I told him when he send his kids money make sure he send it to the mother and then have the mother report that she received the money and he can get credit for it. I also told him to send the money by cashier check or money order that way he has a record of payments, I knew he was not going to do it but I did try to help the young man out. His life was basically over, even if he would had been a lawyer, doctor, or President of the USA, he still would have not made enough because the more you make the more he would have to pay per child. He was a cool guy, I actually like the young man but he was cursed with good looks and that was his down fall, ole and his penis was the reason he was in the position that he was in that day, oh and stupidity, seen to me he would wrapped up the one eyed monster but he did not he just let the horse run free on the range.

He said everywhere he go he meet a woman, I told him he has to start wearing a bag on his head, or at least over one of his heads, he like me as an older brother that was telling him right and helping him. I could honestly say I could relate to him, I know what he is going through, I know what it feel like to be too good looking. I'm cracking up right now and so should you! When I got back in my office I brought up my computer and Googled the Guinness Book of World Records for the most babies by one father and one man had eighty seven babies by a few women, he had about six sets of twins and seven sets triplets and six set of quadruplets. So Theodore Pendergrass had a little ways to go to get the record. Let's move on to the next experience.

WHY!

This next experience is one that will stay with me the rest of my life. This is about a white women who walked in to our office with her little three month old baby girl, the girl was living with a relatives while she was complete her drug rehabilitation she had the child in her early stages of rehab, the state took the baby and gave it to her parents at birth after the hospital made sure the baby was clean from the drugs in her system, her mother looked good until she smiled she had a couple badly decade teeth I thought she was hooked on candy or something but she was in a rehab and she is getting to spend time with her baby now that she been almost a year clean, she is getting close to be able to take her child home with her, she was hooked on meth. That is a huge problem in So-Low; and across the country, this particular drug plagued the White community like crack cocaine plagued the Black and Brown community, but the only difference is now it is effecting the White people they are trying to do everything they can to fight this problem that is plaguing the White community. Well this young lady completed her rehab and was granted a release to go home; she moved into her parent's home for about three more months and worked for them, I attended the court hearing and the mother getting her baby back, all those legal actions was out of my league. Court transactions like that was left up to the people that had legal degrees, background and experience like Attorney's, CPS representatives and Judges but since the child was in my CS caseload, I would attend the hearing sometime when I did not want to stay in the office. I did not really think they should have given the baby back to her so soon because I knew how bad the drug was and what it was doing to people on the streets, but she was

White, need I say more. I had a lot of people in my caseload and I had White friends who children was dealing with the addiction; I knew a lot of them had relapsed at one time or another, she moved out of her parent's home after about three months of living there, they helped her financially get a place and gave her back her baby to raise.

Approximately six months later I received an email from Child Protective Services stating a child in my caseload had passed away, they said the child was approximately sixteen months old, it said the mother was in rehab and upon completion of her rehab stay, she received her child back and she got high on meth and took the baby to a nearby river bank and drowned her in the river, because the baby would not stop crying. The little girl was killed because she would not stop crying; probably because the baby was hungry or wet, whatever the reason is she did not deserve to loss her life, she could have taken the baby to the nearest hospital, fire department or the police station with no questions asked and they would have taken the baby, they said a jogger spotted the little girls legs while running and called the police, the police said they have arrested the mother and have the mother in custody, and she is in the process of being charged with capital murder, she admitted to killing the child, that brought a lot of heat down on So-Low for giving the baby back to the mother, the father was also on meth, he was the one who got the mother hooked on the drugs in the first place. I was glad I did not have anything to do with the mother getting her child back because that would have really taken a toll on me mentally, it took enough of a toll on me by me just seeing the little girl a couple of times in the office and in court. That was one morning I will never forget; a few of the ladies was crying around the office because they had read the story in their local newspapers, and we received the email. This is enough on this story because that child would be around fifteen years old now, I would guess. Again I ask why? Let's move on to another experience this one is too upsetting to me, it burns deep down inside.

153

SAME OLD SEX

We also had gay and lesbian couples adopt children and a few years later they decide the marriage was not working out any longer and they end up divorcing and fighting for custody of the child just like any couple. You would be surprised on how often this happens, I do not know why we are surprise because it is just another two human beings from different backgrounds living together just like a man and a woman. One case I will never forget this lesbian couple was getting a divorce there was a lot of arguing and a lot of crying just like any other couple; this one lesbian couple one is a little white lady, the white lady was nice subdued spoke real soft and a black woman a big sister; she reminded me of Mo'Nique as Nikki Parker in the Parkers, but this woman was what I believe lesbian called her butch, she had short hair and wore jeans, sleeve less t-shirts a leather vest and dingle boots, I am not sure but she might be considered to be a dike. One time she walked into the office and asked for me we was talking custody of the child and the white woman was better off financially, had the better living arrangement for the child the big sister was finding an apartment, she got mad at me and started calling me a sell out and telling me if I was not behind that bullet proof glass she would whoop my ass, she probably would have whoop my ass because she was over six feet and weighted about two hundred and forty five pounces, she also had big feet, big ass titties and arms, she had twenty four inch pythons like Hulk Hogan, she was dirty and also crazy. I laughed at her when she was talking about whooping my ass because I had a lot of people talk about whooping my ass but no one never jumped on me and as long as that did not happen then I do not have to go to jail for trying to kill someone, plus I had that bulletproof glass in between us, she was definitely a heavyweight she was in the same weight class with Big George Foreman, matter of fact I would have paid per-view for that fight. She went into court and started talking about what she was going to do and what she was not going to do and her case came down to her being an alcoholic and her drug use; it was hard seeing them two together because they was so different, I would thing the white woman wanted a man minus the dick, and the black woman was like a man minus the dick, the only reason why I say this is because the sister was so big and the white woman was so little, they looked like a big cement truck and a Mazda Miata, the white woman got custody of the child and the black woman got visitation, they ended up working things out and continue living at two different addresses, the black woman got a good job with a construction company and was able to keep her case current, we became pretty good friends because she would come into the office to make her payments, she would ask for me and I would come out and see her; I would say I'm I due for ass whooping today and we would both start laughing. She ended up being a cool sister, she was just angry at the time, they both were angry, just like any other couple.

We also had a male gay couple adopted a child, this white couple was a trip; because they would argue over everything, one time they walked in to our office and one of the man brought some KFC with him and the other man said did you bring me some chicken; he said yeah I brought you a piece of chicken, he reached in the box and pulled out a piece of original chicken a drumstick, and his partner said we been together for five years and you know I like extra crispy chicken, he said you always do me like that, you never care about me that is why we are divorcing, the partner that liked extra crispy also like his man extra crispy because he would look at me and I would turn my head real fast so he would not put me in a booty trance. I do not have anything against some ones sexual preference but I like woman period! He would look at me like he was undressing me, like I was a sexual object, like I was a peace of extra crispy chicken, I use to feel uncomfortable every time the receptionist called me to help them. My receptionist would call me and say your stuff is in the office again, I use to tell her too call someone else and we would start laughing and I would come down to help them. During their court hearing they both started crying in court and hugging each other talking about how much they love each other and their child, they started kissing on each other, it was hard for me to watch, it was also hard for everyone else in the court room to watch even the women and the judge, some people in the audience was snickering, the attorney's completed the divorce and we set the payment amounts and they walked out of the courtroom together smiling and for this reason everyone thought they was still in love. They actually made their divorce a lot smoother because they agreed to what they was going to get out of the home, visitation, money, and all the other assets they had between each other. Gay couples are here, if you do not like it, that is too bad; they are here to stay, rather you like it or not, everyone will eventually have a gay in their family, if you haven't already, so give them they rights to marriage, medical coverage, just like a heterosexual man or woman couples, remember it is just two human beings living together that may fuck a lot different. So let's move on to another experience.

A REAL MOTHER FOR YA!

For about two years the CSD decided to lease out a portion of our building to another department of So-Low there was about sixty people moved into the section we still had our interviewing area down stairs on the first floor but the other department occupied the majority of the rest of the floor. This department was a woman dominated department with about five men in it; I would sometime walk alongside of their department to go help a walk in client, the employee's started hearing I was a pretty good collector for CS. One day this white woman about thirty two years old walked up to me and said she heard I was one of the better CSO in the department, I told her yeah that's me, she said can you take a look at my case because I have not received a payment in about two years, she said he is on drugs, he started using meth and he has never been the same, I told her to write down her name, account number or social security number with her phone number both cell and business extension on a sticky note and after I help this client I will take a look at her case. I helped my client and stopped by her cubicle and picked up her information; I went back to my office and pull up her case on my computer and started looking over her case she was not in my caseload but from time to time someone else may take your call or walk in if you are busy at the time. I called the woman back and told her I will call her in about a week; I called the father approximately five times and left messages for call back on his answering service. I finally reached the young man; he was about thirty years old, he was homeless at the time, I asked him what is the best address for him, he gave me his parents address, he work odd and end jobs to make money, he live in his truck, I asked him is his truck running, he said not well, I asked

157

where is his truck, he said it is down by the homeless camp near town, the only reason I was able to call him was because he had an Obama phone, Obama had a program that handed out free phones to the poor and the homeless. I sent a sheriff out to serve him so we can get him in to court and depose him, the camp was not far from the court house. He called me after he was served; I told him to come to court, I just wanted to talk to him. He showed for his court hearing because if he did not there would have been a bench warrant issued for a cash bond and potential arrest depending on his prior offensives; he answered present when the judge called roll. I took him in to the court deposition room and asked him about twenty questions he had to answer honestly because the entire court room was sworn in with their right hand raised. It is amazing how many people raise their left hand when the judge tell you to raise your right hand, I always said when they raised their left hand, your other right hand and we would start laughing. The mother showed up for court also because she is a party to the action and she got to sit in the deposition while I was asking the non-custodial parent, the father questions, he was talking about how bad the mother of his kids was treating him, he developed a habit, he said he started using after a few years of living with her, he said he could not take the abuse and he did not want to hit her, he said after he left he tried to see his kids while they was at school, then the mother went out and got a restraining order against him to stay away from her and the kids, he soon lost his job because of his personal issues and everything went downhill from there he was working for a company that could not have any employees with negative marks on their employees or personal history like an arrest, he received a DUI and they found narcotics in his system. I believe it was a finance company he worked for, so he had been homeless and using drugs. He told me he has an opportunity to make some money as a handyman the following week; he said he will be making about two hundred dollars and he would give one hundred and fifty dollars to his wife and kids, I said good, he said he will bring it into the office next week. The following week came and he had a friend drive him to our office to make the payment, while he was sitting in the parking lot he call the mother of his children and told her he was in the parking lot and he will be making the payment in a five minutes. The mother hung up the phone and called the police on him, he was talking to me when the cops rolled up on him and arrested him for violating his restraining order; he could not be within three hundred yards from his wife and kids, I tried to explain to the police he was their making a payment only, but they did not want to hear what I had to say and took him anyway, I walked back into the building and went over to the mothers desk and asked her if she called the police on her husband, she said yes, I told her he was making a payment, she said he could have mailed the payment, I called her a bitch to myself, the father was crying while being arrested, he thought I had something to do with him being arrested, but it was the mother's doing, I knew right then I was not going to help her any longer, after he was released from jail, the mother called me and said he went to his mother home and hung himself in his room, then the mother asked me about how to get his death benefits I told her to call SSA and do not call me any longer. The non-custodial parent called and told me before he passed; he was glad I called instead of one of the women because he said I was the only person who called and made him feel like I really wanted to help him. I told him because I really did want to help him get current or at least get him back on his feet; he said I was the reason why he showed up to court, but instead he might have died thinking I helped set him up, that has always been in the back of my mind since this incident happen, I cannot do anything about it now. I could have slapped the shit out of the mother for doing what she did. The mother called me and said she heard the father owned some property in Arizona two homes, I called the county property tax assessor's office for the state of Arizona but they showed no property ownership under the father's name, I only checked because of his kids, because if they are raised by a mother like her then they may have little chance in life. I learned from this case if you have a person who maybe dealing with mental issues; you should treat them with caution because you never know what type of state of mind or depression they may actually be in. Let me move on because this case piss me off every time I think about it.

INCARCERATION / CLETS/ DNA / EMANCIPATION DAY

I have taken many of trips to the county jail to complete a DNA test on the parents; sometime I would complete a DNA test on just the mother or father and sometime it is on both parents, they would both be incarcerated at the same time the child is born and while a child is growing up. Some woman have a baby and as soon as the baby have been received in the world the nurses let her hold the baby for about five minutes; then they transfer the baby to Child Protective Services (CPS) will leave the new born in the hospital until the doctors decide the child is healthy enough to be transferred to the foster care system and a foster care parent may receive a new born just hours, days or weeks old. CPS will try to keep the child in So-Low but if So-Low does not have the space for the newborn; then they will transfer the newborn to another county, they try to keep the newborn in the nearest county but not all foster care parents can care for a newborn child, foster care parents can choose what age child they prefer to care for, so they maybe a possibility your newborn maybe in a county one hundred miles or further away if a family member does not step up and get custody of your child. The mother will be transferred to county jail or state prison depending on their criminal offense; they will have to serve their time according to the laws of the US courts systems. The mother's or father's family can petition the courts for custody of the child while the child is in the foster care system, if the family petitioners has the proper living facility like a room for the baby, a clean home, drug free, child proof environment, and the recipient is in the position to care for child financially then the courts will allow the relatives to care for the child while the parents are incarcerated, the relative are also subject to surprise inspections at any time CPS see fit. The relative will also have access to welfare assistance to help support the child like free diapers, milk, cheese, EBT card to purchase other necessities a child will need, the parent that is not incarcerated will have to pay for the child's foster care stay and if a relative get custody and want assistance from the father or mother they will have to pay CS, which ever parent who is not incarcerated and does not have the child in their care will have a CS payments each month. Sometime you will have to pay while incarcerated but it is usually put on hold, it depend how long of an incarceration period the person has to complete.

I hated going to the county jail to test the inmates because when I would enter the building walk to the front desk hand the officer my CS ID badge that is hanging around my neck some white asshole cops would ask for my personal driver's license; they would want to run my license number, I use to hate that because they are checking on me to see if I have anything in my history they can arrested or harass me for, everyone else from my office was not scrutinized like the officer scrutinized me. I had officers who seen me on more than one occasion and they continued to run my license; I was just there last week or last month every time I walked in they would run my license, I asked the officers why do they run my license and have to check my license every time I come here, they would say it is standard procedure, I said I hand you my CS identification with my picture on it, my name and other necessary information needed to enter the facility but you always have to run my driver's license number that is not necessary, I would tell them I just seen you last week and they would come up with some bullshit. When I returned to my office I would ask my coworkers who would go to the county jail sometime to do DNA test; do the officers behind the main desk ask for their driver's license every time they go to do DNA test, they would tell me the officers never ask for their license.

I also hated when I had to empty my pockets before entering the jail, I would leave all my items in the car before entering the building because you have to go through a metal detector and after passing through the detector then you have listen to those iron doors slamming behind you, you hear this loud clanking noises as the doors close and lock, you know you are not going anywhere, I would have to walk through about four different iron doors slamming behind me before I would reach the inmates area in So-Low's jail it is not like most jails and prisons in the state of California, the majority of the inmates is Mexican and White because they do not have a large African American population incarcerated in the facility. There is not a large population of African American in the county; I would walk in the jail facility and see about two to five inmates who look like me, if there was a large population of African American I am sure the police in this area of the state would hurry up and even the incarceration score, I heard most of the African Americans who is incarcerated in So-Low Jail Facility is incarcerated because they were pulled over while traveling through the county, they are pulled over and the officer find some reason to incarcerated the driver or passengers in the vehicle. This information was not surprising to me because of the way they treated me when I enter the facility and I am an officer of the county, and they continually running my license.

See the Polices and all other law enforcement agency in the state of California and all the other states in the United States of America have a centralize communication system; California has the CLETS system which stands for the California Law Enforcement Telecommunication System, this system is the computer board you see sitting near the dashboard in every law enforcement vehicle. The officer would run your license plate number while following you and the computer system will give the office everything about the registered owner of the vehicle except for what size drawls he or she is wearing. We have the CLETS system in our office and I have a sign on; but I would never walked within fifteen feet of that system after I was trained on it, if they saw me anywhere near the system half my coworkers and every supervisor and manager would want to know what I am doing on this system. Is it curiosity or is it just plain old prejudicial tendencies you can choice, I already know, I set at this system one time during my twenty years employment history and that was during my training, I never set at this system again, if you ran your friends name in the system and he or she does not have a CS case this is grounds for immediate termination, they was watching me like I was in a Target store, like a hawk, like I was a black man walking alone in a rich white neighborhood day or night, I would not have been surprise if a buzzer would go off if I sat at the system, you definitely had to be white to get on the CLETS system without being question. It got to the point where; I forgot my sign on for the system, I had it written down in one of three old password books in my desk.

Back to the DNA testing in the county jail; I would complete the test on the inmate in the medical area of the jail or in their cells, I hated doing the test in their cells because some cell had bars and some inmates was housed in a cell with a big iron door, I believe it had a ten by ten inch window in the middle of the door those was the inmates I believe was on suicide watch, I would think to myself "damn it is hard to breath in here and you talking about anxiety, my anxiety was high and I was going home!" I kept thinking I do not want to be locked up, I do not want to be locked up, I would be scared straight every time I walk in there, and there was an armed sheriff posted outside the cell! I would have the inmate swab him or herself instead of me actually sticking the swab stick in their mouths, I would demonstrate how I want them to swab their mouths with an imaginary swab, I have protective gloves and mask on but I did not give damn, I was not sticking nothing in or near their mouths because you can catch all types of shit like Hepatitis A B or C I believe C is the worst it is also known as HCV this is a disease that attack your liver, most people do not know they have it, about three million people have it at present, I made sure I kept my distance while doing these test, I watch them and made sure it was done correctly, I made sure that they was rubbing the two swabs on the enter jaw in the back of their mouths and the swab had plenty of saliva on the Q-tips portion of the swabs, I took the swabs and put them back in the individual sleeves that accompanied the swab from the official DNA Lab facilities and labeled the package correctly, when I return to our office the same day, we will overnight the test back to the DNA facility to complete examination and they will forward the result of the test within three days. Then we will have potential father, sometimes mother and father will come in to the office, sometime if the mother and father does not get alone we would have them come in at separate times or if the person want the results over the phone we will give the results that way, they also get result letters mailed to their place of residence. You are the father! Working for the CSD is like having your own Maury Povich Show the only difference is I was the host and no audience, I got to say, you are the father or you are not the father! I would see some men jump for joy because they were not the father and some men will jump for joy because they were the father, it goes both ways the excitement, I also see the women's reaction when the child is not the child of the man she named to be the father, after she quit crying and the father of her last two kids knew this child cannot be his child because he is a white man with blond hair and the baby has dark tent to his or her skin color and head full of black curly hair or maybe the child might have Asian eyes, it could be a number of reasons that will make the father belief that the child is not theirs. Then the mother has the task to name another possible father; I had one woman who had to name seven different possible fathers before we located the actual father, after we located him he stated he will not stay with her but he was going to take care of his son, she had about three kids already. I also had the fathers who have a handicap child and will give them the extra love they need and some father do not want to have anything to do with their handicap child. One thing about men I notice during my work tenure; a man will leave the home without his children and go live with another woman and help her raise her kids, her kids already have father, so Homey don't play that! Every father have to take care of their own kids, I had men literally cry, because they have to pay the mother of their kids, you would be surprise how often this happens, some man leave home and forget their kids name literally and try their best not to claim them, but Homey don't play that and neither does the states.

I had kids find out about the emancipation laws and want to be separated from their parents; I had one young man about sixteen years old, get mad at his parents and wanted to seek emancipation from them. He came into the office and our receptionist called and asked me to talk to him. I came down stairs; he walked up to my booth and said he want to be emancipated from his parents, I told him I am not able to talk to him without a parent present because he is a minor. I asked if he talk to his parents about his emancipation request, he said no, I told him he might want to talk to them, I told him he was going to have to go to through court system to complete the emancipation process, he said I have to go through the court system! I told him yes, you cannot just wake up and say you are emancipated, I told him on his eighteenth birthday he can do that, but any time before, he will have to go through the courts. I told him on his eighteen birthday there is a good chance he might still need his parents. I asked him if he had a job, he said he was looking for job, I asked him if he is being abused, he said they yell at him, I said did you deserve to be yelled at, he said I did not clean my room or complete my homework, I said other than you giving them a reason to yell at you, and those are reasons to yell at you. I told him do not get mad because they do not want their child to grow up and be a dummy or a child who does not clean up behind his or herself. He said you sound like my parents, I said because I have two of you at my house and I wish they would file for emancipation so I would not have to take care of their asses. I leaned over the counter; asked the young man to lean forward and I told the young man real low to take his ass home before I yell at him, he started laughing, I then said tell your parents you love them when you get home, because they love you, Knucklehead! He left the office and went to school!

NO! NOT AGAIN!

This next experience is about a white man who had a good construction job; he was a manager making good money he had four girls who he loved and they loved him, and he paid his child support on time. Our receptionist called me and asked me to come down and assist him with his case, I called the father up to the interviewing booth and he sat down, I reviewed his case and I said what is the problem, you are current. He said I know; he said I need to talk to you about something else, he said you have to stop my ex-wife from moving everywhere he moves, I said what do you mean, he said I have moved five times and every time he moved, she moves her and their daughters in the same apartment complex because she does not want him to have any privacy, she would tell him he is going to help raise his kids every day and he married her, he is going to be around his kids rather he want to or not, if he had a woman friend by his apartment she would come over and start an argument with his woman friend, she would start telling his woman friends he has four girls in this apartment right over there and she would point at her apartment. He was in his early fifties; he had the lead singer of the Bee Gees look, head full of blond hair and a well-groomed salt and pepper beard and every time he moved his ex-wife move to the same area or complex and the reason she was able to move every time was because of the amount of money he was paying her for CS, he was as frustrated as a person can be, he said is there anything we can do to help him. I told him I cannot help him; we cannot stop her from moving, I said he can get a restraining order or he can have us take his case back into court and he can try to get the judge to add a stipulation to his judgement where the mother cannot move into the same housing complex as the father, I told him I never heard of a judge actually doing something like that, because I know that is violating one of her amendment rights, I said I am not attorney so do not go by my words, I told him to go see our family law facilitator and talk to them because the family law facilitator is an attorney who is employed by the county but is free to you because you have a CS case, maybe they can recommend an action he can take. He said thanks. The next day the mother walked in our office and asked for me, when I called her to the interviewing booth, she walked up and she scared me, she did not have any makeup on and she scared the shit out of me, she had let herself go, she walked in looking like former professional heavyweight boxer Randall "Tex" Cobb, or WWF wrestler "Moon dog" Mayne, she walked in with her four girls and she was out of shape, she looked like she was pretty at one time in her life, but now she did not give a damn about her appearance at this time, I could see why he left her, she also had a bad attitude, she was mad at me because he told her what suggestions I gave him the day before. I told her I am just doing my job, I said that is the reason she is receiving her support, because I am doing my job, she said she would appreciated if I would stay the hell out of her business other than the money, she told me not to give her another reason to come down or else she is going to kick my ass! We looked at each other in the eyes for about ten second and I said ok! Shit if we would have stared at each other for another five seconds, I might have peed on myself. She was definitely big enough to whoop my ass, I was waiting for her to call me out of my name and I was going to take it, I was not going to say shit, not one thing. After she left I was like: I would have whooped that bitch ass, she does not know who she is fucking with, she don't scare me, not the man, I'm the MAN! I was glad she was gone, a couple of my co-workers was cracking up because they heard the entire incident, my receptionist told me she thought she was going to have to call the

169

police to pull that bitch off me. I called the father when I got back to my office and said to him, why did he tell her what I said to him and he cracked up, I told him he almost got my ass kick this morning, he said you met her, I said yeah, she came in this morning looking like the abominable snowman in the old Christmas television show, he started laughing, he said he loved her, but she quit taking care of herself and he got tired of listening to her shit, he said he is going to get a restraining order. I told him thanks for the ass whooping! We cracked up, I never heard from them again, that is how it be, one day people are in your life and once you take care of their case, you may not see or hear from them again or until they need assistance on their case again. Now you see them, now you don't!

HOMELESS

We have a ton of homeless cases especially now a days with price of living going up by the minute; there are more and more homeless children in our world, the more difficult the USA make it for people to survive in our country the worse the homeless situation becomes. I have assist thousands of homeless people with their CS; I would help them locate jobs by building a relationship with the temporary job agencies around the county, because it could be a number of reasons why a person become homeless, no job, mental illness, abuse as a child, terrible parenting, incarceration, drug use, sexual offender, laziness, sexual abuse or just plain ole bad luck through life to name a few. Barack Obama made a move for the homeless population and it made it a lot easier to communication with them, he gave out free cell phone to everyone who could not afford them, the homeless called them The Obama Phones. There are millions of children sleeping on the streets in the cold every night around our country, if their parents fail so does their children.

The foster care system is definite needed in our country it can be good and bad for the child or children, foster care parents can choose what age child they want to care for, so if you have multiple children there is a good possible the children could be separated so the child will go from an environment with their brothers or sisters to an environment where the child do not know anyone in the home, sleeping, eating, playing with strangers. You do not have a clue who your child is living with, my kids would tell me I could not whoop them, because they will call the police on me, I told them go ahead call the police, the police would put you and your sister in foster care and instead of you two sleeping with your TV and Play Stations, you will be sleeping in a room with a bully, a gay kid, and another kid with a helmet on his head, I told my kids you better thank God for their living situation, because there is a lot of children who are a lot less fortunate then they. These situations where a child could be in four or five different living environments could be devastating to a child mental and physical development and some children has been in so many foster cares, when they turn eighteen they are release in to society with no jobs, no home, no means of supporting themselves this is a guarantee road map for failure. Then some of the foster children will run from every foster care facility where they are placed, then the county have to try to locate child and put he or she back into the same facility or a different facility so the child can escape again, one reason they may continue to escape the facility is because they are in search of their siblings, their parents, or just plain ole safety. I heard stories where foster parents was beaten up by a foster care child or a foster care child is molested by the foster parents male or female. Some foster children luck up and find someone to really take an interest in their well-being, in order for this to happen the foster child must be willing to trust this particular adult and realize the adult truly care about them. Once you gain the child's trust it is a must situation you do not lose their trust, because if you lose their trust you may never get it back, because the child has already lost trust in so many adults, it will be next to impossible to restore the relationship and who could blame the child, they had their parents, relatives, social workers, courts, foster parents all fail to protect them, they did not ask to born in this world, they did not ask to be kicked around from home to home, they did not ask to not be loved, they was born in this world to bring joy in their parent's life, it is their parent responsibility to educated and turned them into productive citizens, they was born in this world by the grace of God. There is a lot of good parents who cannot have children because of health reasons and then there are some parents that is not ready or should not have children, whatever the reason you have a moral obligation to do everything possible to care for your child and anyone else's child; children is the future of the world, they are the next generation and the next ancestors in the family tree of yours and my life, they must be cherished, loved and valued, they cannot be forgotten, overlooked or abused, it is lonely on the street for a child without much knowledge of the world, it is like a terrarium sitting on a table as people walk bye and glance at it, but few stop and wonder how the plants got in the bottle and how they are watered and nourished, people just keep on walking and forget about the beauty the terrarium brings to the world, this happens with homeless children we forget how the child got in this position and how a child can bring beauty and contribute to the world if properly nourished mentally and physically, every child can contributed to this world and we cannot continue to just walk on by and pay no attention to the weak and vulnerable, they are there so pay attention to them, say hi, give them some money, give them some food, give them some respect, respect does not cost anything, it is free, give them hope, try it next time it might make you feel good inside. I had a sixteen year old girl walk into our office she stated she is pregnant and she is homeless she was just about four months pregnant, she was able to get enough money together to get a pregnancy test and take the test. She said the father is an older man who raped her while she was living on the streets, I asked where is her parents, she said they kicked her out of the home, I told her well we have to get you back in her parent's home. I told her she has not had the baby, so there is nothing I can do as far as opening up a case, I said you have to have the baby first. I called one of our social workers and had representative come get the white young lady from our office, I told her after she have her baby then we will get the father. She and her parents contacted me after the baby was born and I had the father served and pulled him into court, slapped him upside his head for raping her and then the law incarcerated him for raping her, having sex with a minor and impregnating her, when he get out he has a child he will have to take care of, because she was on state assistance with the child so he will owed the state. Let's move on from this sick motherfucker!

PROFESSIONAL

While I was in the CSD we had a few professional athlete's get caught up in the CSD, I will never forget when we had a beautiful Mexican woman walked in to our office, my receptionist called my office and asked me to help her. I went down to the interviewing booth and spoke with the young lady; she stated she want to open up a case for CS. She met a professional athlete while on vacation in Mexico; they had sex and she became pregnant, I am sure this athlete was not aware of the Mexican's women religious beliefs prior to having sex with the woman, plus she was very fine. He did not know most Mexican's did not believe in birth control and he had unprotected sex with the woman, they produce a child he did not want and he was refusing to pay support until we completed the DNA test, which determined he was the father of the child. We had to track the young man down to get him to complete the DNA test, he would leave town and make it as difficult as possible for our office to complete the test, I contacted his agent and he released some of the athlete's personal information concerning his income, taxes and contracts once we determined he was the father. I forwarded his file to our intake department and when it was time for the enforcement portion of the case to be done this athlete had to pay the mother thirty thousand dollars a month CS for one child. You remember in one of my earlier chapters I stated the more money you make the more money you will have to pay well this is a perfect example of what I was saying, thirty thousand dollars was more than a lot of people made in a year. This athlete was pissed when he had to pay this amount, I educated the athlete on the CS and let him know if he received a pay cut we can recalculate the support once a year, I also told him CS could go up or down depending on his salary, I let him know his CS can also go down depending on how much visitation he has with their son, at this time the professional athlete did not want to have anything to do with his child or mother of their child, he was pissed off and felt he was trapped by this woman. I could see how he felt trapped especially after he had sex one time with the woman or at least that is what he told me, but everyone know it only take one time and your life could be totally changed just like that and just that fast, I told him if he let the woman move in with him then he will not have to pay her but she will have access to all his money, he said fuck that! I told the young athlete he needs to start wrapping his whacker up because there is a lot women out there who will get pregnant on him as soon as they find out how deep his pockets is, that was my way of pulling the young man's coat tail on this issue. I also told him if he has another child to let us know so we can modify his case; I still see him on television from time to time depending on what sport and team I am watching, that was last time I spoke to this this young man. Let's move on to the next situation.

GIVE ME SOME SKIN

In So-Low they have a lot of races ass people who live in this rural area of the state; there are mobile homes parks, cheap hotels, motels and homeless camps built off the side of the highways which surrounds the county, they have a skin head and white supremacy population in the area, I would see, I hate Obama signs, confederate flags, bigotry symbol, Neo Nazis symbols could be found on peoples clothes, homes, car and trucks, I work there for twenty years and only stated out late night two times one time is for our Christmas party. I knew there was skin heads in the county but I did not know exactly where they lived, I just thought they lived around me, I did not really know the difference between the two groups, all I knew was they did not like my ass, as far I was concern that was enough for me.

I had one white boy walk in to our office he was about six–two and approximately three hundred and fifty pounds; he was just released from state prison so the receptionist called me to help him, he had a bald head and had a bunch of racist tattoos on his head, one of the tattoos signs on his head was the German Swastika symbol. I called him up to the window and he walk over to receptionist and asked if he could have another representative and the receptionist was a Mexican woman she knew what he was asking, she told him no, Harry is all we have right now, she said he is one of our better officers I really did not want to help his races ass anyway, so he came and set down and was looking at me like he wanted to kill me, I was looking back at him like I will fuck you up if you came across the counter, I hate races ass motherfuckers like this white boy sitting in front of me, either you are an asshole or you are not in my book. Before I started help him with his case I told the white boy he could wait for someone else if he like, I told him I am not to particular happy about helping his ass. I said you do not like me because my skin color, he said right, he said you and your people are trying to take our country from the white race. I said where is your parents from, he said I am Irish, I said who did your parents take this country from, last I looked I am not in Ireland, he said the white race is superior, I said superior to who, he said to the black race, I said if the Irish people are superior to blacks, I guess it would be more of you in the NBA, just to fuck him. I said you do not know me, he said I do not need to know you; to know you are no good. I said you feel you are superior to me? He said he is superior to me, I said you may think you are superior me, but you are not, I said you have the right to think what you want but you are no better than I am, I said a matter of fact I am superior to you because I am the person who is handling your case, he said are you threating me, I said yeah I am, he said fuck you, and I looked at him back in his eyes and said fuck you too motherfucker real low. I said you want to call me a nigger, he said yeah, I said call me nigger please and I won't do shit for you. I said so what you need, he said he need his license so he can get a job, I said you have any money, he said I just got released from prison he only had two hundred dollars that he got from his parents he could put down. I told him I need three hundred down and he was starting to look all sad and I started laughing and I said I told you I am superior to your ass. I said I will take the two hundred and I will released his license for thirty days and explained all the rules and regulations, I told him to call me as soon as he get a job, I will issue a wage assignment, I told him to make sure he call me when he get a job, because if he does not the system will pick him up and issue the wage assignment and he going to wish he talk to me. I said if he miss a payment his license will be suspended again, I said that will give him another chance to come see me, I said you do not want to see

178

me again, I also said get rid of some of the hatred in your heart, I said because he will never be superior to me as long as he has that hatred in him and even then he still won't be superior to me or the black race. When he got ready to leave I started singing "Say it loud I am black and I am proud" by James Brown and started laughing again, now get the hell on out of here, that was fun can I do it again, believe me I seen plenty of those ass holds come into the office. Hating someone because of their skin color, can I ask you something? What kind a shit is that? Dumb motherfucker! Let's move on!

TWO SISTERS

This young white boy approximately twenty years old with a happy go lucky mood, long sandy blond hair, smelling like weed and do not have a care in the world until now, he reminded me of "Spicoli" in the movie "Fast Time At Ridgemont High" walked in the CSD our receptionist called me to help him, I came down stairs to help him. I called him up to the interviewing booth and set down, he said he was told by his mother to go to the CSD and open up two CS cases. I said to him you have a baby by two different women, he said yes, I said what is their names and he said Christy and Brandi Watson, I said both of them have the same last names, he said yeah they are sisters, I said what you talking about Willis? I said they are sisters, he said yes, I said Black women? He said no, I said biological sisters? He said yes. I said you was laying up with biological sisters and they both got pregnant, he said yes. I asked him if the sisters knew he was laying up with both of them, he said no because he was seeing them at different times and places. I said are they the same age, he said Brandi is one year younger than Christy, they was nineteen and eighteen years old; the kids was born half-brother and sister. That is when his mother walked in the office and came over to the booth, a nice looking older white woman, she came from work because I could tell how she was dressed. I told her your son was telling me about his situation, she said yeah he does not have a clue what he got himself into, I said I know, we started to laugh, I told her he will find out in a hurry, she said I know. I asked the young man, what the father of the two young ladies think of him knocking up his two daughters, he said their father told him if he see him around his daughters again he will personally kill him and he will be paying for both babies, one

180

daughters had a boy and the other daughter had a girl the babies was born about two months a part their father told him he will pay for both the kids one way or another. I asked the young man do he really believe their father, the young man said their father own about twenty guns and rifles, he said he believes what he is saying, I said I do too. He said that is why I am here, he asked if he can open a CS case instead of the mother's, I said yes he can, he said that way he can get money to the kids. His mother said she will be helping him pay for the kids until he get a good job, I told him by opening up a CS case we will be taking the money direct out of his check and he will have to pay CS until the kids are eighteen years old and until they graduate high school, also he will get visitation rights with his kids, his mother was happy for that because she want to see her grandkids and have a relationship with them. I gave him two case opening packets to open his cases, they complete packets and turned it in, I asked the young man do he want a DNA test, I told him he can get the test completed for free within in the next thirty days if he turn the test down he will have to pay out of pocket for any future tests, his mother said let's do the DNA test to be sure, her son agreed, so we complete the test that day on the father, we opened his cases and within the next couple weeks we completed DNA test on both babies and both mother's, both results came back" he was the father". Once we finalized the young man case in court I never seen him or his mother, or the baby momma's after the judgement was entered on both cases, I did see the father of the young ladies in court and yeah he did look like the type of man who would have no problem popping a cap in the young man's ass. Let's move on to the next crap!

UNION MY ASS

These days some unions is a waste of money, I was member of one of those union, I was a member of the Stationary Engineers Union in this area, Local Nineteen it was a worthless ass union, their head office was located in another major city. I paid my union membership dues for twenty years, I believe we was paying sixty a month or sixty dollars a check I cannot remember the exact amount. All I know is this union was the weakest union I have ever been associated with, we had this union representative who was deep in So-Low back pocket. So-Low had this white boy in his forties in their back pocket that way it was easier for him to kiss their ass; he was a terrible representatives, I hated giving them my money he never came through for his members, I stop going to meeting after about three years. Each time I had a problem with So-Low and each time I reached out for help, the counties ended up treating me exactly like they see fit. Every time we fought for something and made progress on an issue he would give up something that we fought for in the past, I was trying to explain to him we should not be giving up anything after we make progress on issue, you will realize what I mean as you read on, we would take two steps forward and one step back every time he negotiate a contact. We are going to call him James to protect guilty. I remember one time the employee all got tired of his bullshit and started trying to terminate our association with local nineteen when the final vote was tallied our co-workers failed to stick together I voted to terminate our relationship with this Local because they failed to protect my ass or anyone else ass. I remember I was in an office with majority white and Hispanic women co-workers, they was scared to stick the together, there was a white woman who lead the charge and she had researched other unions and spoke to different representatives about representing us but some of the women in the office lost their nerves and voted against leaving, they was scared of So-Low and what they might do, and they would have not done anything especially to the white employees. As you read on you will find out exactly what I been telling you about our wonderful union and our fantastic union representative sorry ass!

IS THAT ENOUGH, NO!

I want everybody to sit down and just think about all the bad shit that goes on in this world; some of the shit might make its way next door to you, just imagine a five mile radius all around your home, you do not know what the hell is going on in these homes around your neighborhood. Now a days you cannot let your child or children play in front of your home without proper supervision twenty four-seven, you let your child play out front of your home without watching them, there is a good chance your child could be taken or abused. I have seen lots of children come through the child support division that look like they might be abused or did they just fall at school. There is a wide arrange of child abuse going on in this wonderful world of ours. There is physical abuse where an adult has done physical harm to the child by hitting the child with their hands, feet, biting or using an object to inflict pain like a cigarettes, belts, branches to apply punishment to a child.

There is mental abuse used on children on a daily bases some people know they are abusing the child, they are doing it purposely; there are others who do not realize they are degrading the child mentally and next thing you know this abuse has been going on for years and you fail to realize the abuse you have inflexed on your child's self-esteem, confidence, pride, where he actually feel and think he is dumb or stupid because you have called him it so many times in his or her life, I am not going to tell you I have never called my kids dumb or tell my kids that was stupid, because kids will do dumb and stupid shit during their life, but it is just as important to pat them of the back and give them encouragement when they do well in life, you cannot degrade a child on a consistent bases they need positive feedback also.

Child neglect goes on in this world on a daily bases, there are children who is locked in closets or a basements right now cold in the dark not receiving life's necessities and proper facilities needed to raise a child, not being made to get up and go to school to grab education, allowing a child to stay home cut classes and not eating a hearty and healthy meal daily this is the parents responsibility to make sure a child is properly nourished and have his or her basic living needs to help the child grow up to be a healthy young adult. There are different types of neglect physical, educational, medical and emotional just to name a few.

Sexual abuse is another form of child abuse that is running rapid in our world, you find sick adults who is taking advantage of children all over the world. They are being sexually abused in homes, on the streets of our country, and even in churches around the world which in my opinion is one of the worst thing a person can do to a child under the Lord's watchful eye, sexual abuse can cause a child a life time of medical issue along with psychological, and physical issues. This unlawful act will land you on a permanent web page called Megan's Law you will be obligated to register as a sex offender for the remainder of your life, every time you move to another state or county you must register with that county in whatever state you choose to live in within forty eight hours or you can be arrested and charged with failing to register as a sex offender and will be sentence to prison, you also cannot be within three hundred yards of any school or you can be arrested, there are approximately nine hundred thousand registered sex offend in the USA today and counting.

Abandonment is another way you can embed the notion that a child is not wanted. A child need to know he or she is loved and wanted, for a child to not be wanted is a feeling that will follow the child the rest of their lives, you see other kids being hugged, kissed, shown affection from their mother, father or family members that could destroy a child that is not receiving any affection or love at all, the lack of love and trust is the worst words an abandon child can hear. Mothers and fathers attending school meetings, programs, sporting events and you have another child who do not have a grandmother or grandfather or any adult who is willing to make this child their center attention. A child being left on a door step of a strangers home, family members home, fire station, police department, hospital, a bus stop or a garbage dumpster; just think if your parents just got tired of you one day and gave you away while you was a child you will never be mentally, emotionally and physically able to deal with this issue, you will always wonder why this happen to you, why your parents did not want you any longer, what did you do to deserve this treatment from your parents. The word trust will never be a part of your vocabulary again; you will no longer trust any adult or authority figure.

There are signs a child has been abused in some way or another; depression sets in, delayed or inappropriate behavior, no or low self-esteem, social withdrawal, and avoidance of certain situations like not wanting to go to school or enter a certain room because this is where the abuse has taken place. In these cases Child Protective Service also known as CPS can come to your home at any time of day or night and take your child or children out of your home; if there is any type of unsafe environment, if a family member call and report you, a nosey neighbor call and report you, CPS can come and remove the children from your home and guess who is responsible for the children expenses while they are being held in foster care, you, me, and everyone else in one way or another. The parent will be billed for their expenses the same way a parent would be billed for child support; if the parent is not employed or is on public assistance then we are all on the hook for the child's expenses, that is why it is called public assistance because the public is footing the bill in the form of taxes. CPS must agree with the reported claim of abuse before they will remove the child, if they do not see signs of abuse or unsafe environment they can also leave the child, if they do not agree with the person who call in the report, in all case there is an armed police officer present at the time of the visit to prevent violence from breaking out or the child being injured while being removed, this happens in our wonderful world on a daily basic within all nationalities in this land, I believe there are more white people on public assistance per capita in the USA today, I believe I heard that fact during my career in this industry.

There is a huge problem when it comes to child trafficking in our country, our children are being taken at an alarming rate each year. Children are being abducted daily in the USA, they are being transported to other states and country, for what I understand more children are being abducted in the state California more than any other state in the country, Texas is next. Children are abducted and sole in to slave labor and prostitution both male and female thousands of children are never seen again, one out five humans abducted is children, they are drugged and sent out to beg on the street, child phonograph, and child labor. This is a problem the USA need to put more effort into because we need to protect our children they are greatest and most valuable resources, they are our future. Next crap!

CO-WORKERS

While working for the DA Office in the CSD for twenty years I had plenty of co-workers during my time of employment, some who have worked with me my entire career and some worked with me half my career, some worked just a couple years with me during the end of my career. During my time of employment I had coworkers said cruel things to me and I had co-workers who would never say anything cruel to me; I tried to be courtesy to all my co-workers the majority of my co-workers was women, so I made it point of treating them with respect all the time. I treated each woman in the office with the respect they deserved, the women I can play around with we joked and had fun, there was some woman like talking shit with me and threaten to whoop my ass, there was some who did not have much to say to me and I kept our communication down to a minimal business only, there was approximately seven or eight gentlemen in the office at the time of my departure we all got along pretty good. I have a lot of co-workers who I enjoyed working with like this one Mexican young lady who ended up leaving and moving down south with her and her family, we are still good friends through technology, she use to call me froggy because of my voice. I had another Mexican woman who is beautiful and had about six kids from about three different men and she is still exceptionally fine she ended up leaving the CSD also, she was happy to be leaving So-Low CSD even though she still live and raising her children in the So-Low. I had a co-worker who had a beautiful heart, a woman with a strong religious base, she had went through tragedy that is unimaginable for one person to handle, no one should never have to go through the tragedy and pain she had to endure, with the Lord's assistance she was able to make it through all her heart ache and ended up retiring a few years prior to my departure. One of my co-worker and friends was a Mexican woman who served in the military and adopted an autistic child who showed me plenty of love over the years; I have known her and her child since she was a baby, I believe her and I have the same date of birth. I also had another co-worker who was a very beautiful heavy set young lady with a good heart she has always worked hard to get what she got, she drove a nice car and was in her early twenties I called her my apple pie and she did not mined my nickname at all for her, she was just starting her own family right about the time I was retiring I am sure she is good mother and wife.

I also had a white co-workers; I asked one white woman have she ever gone out with a black man, she told me the one black man she went out with did not smell good, so she refuse to go out with another black man. I told her she had three kids with three white man none of them stated with her; but she is too good to go out with a black man, this particular woman was a nice looking white young lady none of her baby daddy's was paying, she came to my office and asked me if I would look at her cases and see if I could help her get some money from their father's. I told her I would take a look at her cases; I got all three of them working and paying their support, she was happy I was able to help her get some money, but was too good to go out with me or any other black man, we stink! She was that type of white woman who would go out with a black man as long as her friends or family do not see her, the type of white woman who will wake up the next morning and not remember what she done the night before, when she know damn well she was freaked up and down and all the way around, I cannot remember My Ass! I still considered her a good friend as we worked together, like I said before I have always had a soft spot in my heart for single parents because I know how hard it is to keep surviving in this world as a single

189

parent, so I did not let her stupidity come between our friendship and me educating her on diversity, I also had a chance to watch her three kids get older and becoming good young adults but her youngest child might end up incarcerated if she do not whoop his ass or some kid in his school don't kick his little ass, his dad was a racist he thought I was laying up with all the women and the mother of his child, she must have forgot to tell him all black man smell bad, because he did not like me and I knew it, I also knew she liked me as a person deep down inside and she knew I was missed treated while employed at So-Low.

There was a pretty and fine middle age white woman who worked with me; she enjoy piecing and tattoos, she was cool had a good attitude toward the black race, I believe she was born in the southern California area, I believe she had gone out with black men before and we use to have some funny conversation in her office, just talking about current events, sports teams and families she watched my kids grow up and I watched her two kids become a young adults, her children was older them my kids. I use to jokingly say to her "you want me don't you?" and she use to say "Harry I want you like a hold in my head" we use to crack up laughing, we had a good time and good conversations, I enjoyed her company, she was a single parent she was fine well-groomed nice looking lady despite all the tattoos, I use to say all those tattoos is some freaky shit, we would laugh, she also had bedroom eyes, her eyes was a bluish grey color, she was one of the few women in the office who showed me a little compassion, she knew the treatment I received was unfair and management knew it also, but majority of the women did not care, she would kid around with me while showing me a little compassion. Next!

One of my female co-workers told me she does not allow blacks in her car; I said no problem and got in my own car, drove to my destination. She knew what she said was fuck up and immediately after she made the statement she realized how fucked up her statement was, but it was too late; I was thinking to myself while I was driving to my destination these motherfuckers out here is crazy, even the Mexicans are prejudice toward blacks as we continue to work together she started seeing I was a cool and respectable man, so she decided to apologize to me approximately six months later, once she apologized she eventually started talking to me more and we became pretty good friends. She said her and her man was into pain while making love, she said they like using tools, toys, handcuffs, whips, collars and ropes, I use to tell her you and your husband is a couple "freaks" we would crack up. I told her I bet their love sessions look like a crime scene at the end; I asked her have they every drew blood on each other she said sometimes, I asked her what is this love style called she said society call it S & M and B & D that was one of the first times I had ever heard of these methods of love making, I just called it love making and freaking or fucking, I had heard through the grapevine it was freaks like them in the world, but what are the chances of one being across the office from me "lucky me." I asked her what did the initials stand for she said S&M stands for Sadism and Masochism, B&D Bondage and Discipline, I asked her have she ever left her husband tided up while she was at work, she said she thought about it a few times, I thought it was funny she said she would grab her whip and start beating him and he spanked her sometime but most of the time she whooped him, I told her she is the only woman I know who walked in the house and literally start beating her husband down, I said most men take their ass whooping in some other way or another, I would say "that is some freaky shit"! She stated they also have a couple of sex machines, I said like Michael Jackson album, she said no, you know different sex machines the man and the woman can lay on in different positions while having sex, I said you have an adjustable bench that goes up and down, she said it twist in different angles also, I would say

191

can I watch and we would start laughing! I would see her husband at work sometimes and think you are a freaky little young motherfucker, they both was younger than I by approximately fifteen years. I asked have their three kids ever seen their toys and machines and she said they keep it in a trunk in their closet locked up, she said the machines fold up in the trunk, I said the machines come with a trunk, she said they purchased the trunk at Walmart, I said I guess you picked up the whip cream and chocolate syrup while at Walmart, she said yes, and we cracked up. That is some freaky shit! But to each its own! We still are pretty good friends and she even allowed me to ride in her car a couple times, lucky me! After all that freaky shit, I was not sure if I even wanted to get in her car, after all the freaking in different positions, freaking in the car would be practice for those two. Next!

ATTORNEYS AND PROCESS SERVER

I also had a pretty good relationship with our attorney's in the office beside the racist attorney I spoke of at the beginning of this book, we had a number of attorneys in our division, we also had a few investigators who came through our office, beside the investigator that was investigating me earlier in the book. Most of the attorneys and investigators was good people they was there to take care of the children in our caseloads, the children in other counties and state's caseload, because all counties worked together on the same statewide computer system, we are out to complete the same goals and that is to collect money for the children, help custodial and noncustodial parents and protect the children of our country. I worked with a number of attorneys during the course of my twenty years of employment at So-Low CSD most of them was good people we had a white female attorney a young lady who had a great attitude, she was never to business to help me or anyone else in our office, she would give us her opinion, legal expertise and different ways to solve an issue. She was a fine red head woman who was just starting her family, she had a couple red headed kids that looked just like her, she was always courtesy to everyone and willing to help everyone she encountered I enjoyed conversing with her over cases, she knew I was not the best at completing some of the legal documents for court, so she would either help me complete the documents or complete it herself, I had nothing but the upmost respect for her, I consider her a good five day a week friend and bought girl scout cookies from her daughters every year.

Toward the end of my career we had a new lead attorney come in to our office; he was a white guy and former lead criminal law attorney in

So-Low, he moved over to the CSD because he was tired of sending all the minorities to prison, so he move to the civil division to ease his mine a little. I enjoyed working with him he was born on the east coast our football teams was rivals, our baseball team was rivals, our basketball team was rivals, most of the time his football and baseball team beat my teams, but not his basketball team I won those games, we made friendly wagers like candy bars or a soda, sometime our coworkers would have a football pool going around the office, we did not have any real bets because he made more money than I did, so it was no need for me to be giving him all my money. I use to tell him he was like a bodyguard "concrete heart cannot hold no love" that saying is from an old reggae song by a group called Steel Pulse, I use to listen too in my younger days, I came to that conclusion after he gave me permission to serve this non-custodial parent at a funeral of one of his family members, in his defense we had been trying to get this father serve for a while and was having a real difficult time getting the service documents in his hand, because he refuse to answer his door when the sheriff or our process server went to his place of resident, I thought it funny because he was willing to do it, but I was not going to set the service up without talking to our director and she said "hell no" so we did not do it, our lead attorney and I cracked up, you have to remember our lead attorney came from the criminal division. I still liked him as a man because he was fair to everyone and he was just a good person, and father who like to laugh and had a good attitude for the most part, he was like me in some ways he would do what it would take to collect the support, Like one time we did a (QDRO) Qualified Domestic Relations Order this is a method of collecting money through a person retirement, pension, 401k, profit sharing, federal government, military, plan administrators and other business entities. He like me as an officer because he knew I was like him in some ways because I just wanted to collect money for

194

the child, we very seldom disagreed on how to handle a case he liked my innovated ideals like when I approached him about a case, the non-custodial parent was a dentist and I told him we should seize all his precision metals then he would have to pay his support or he would not be able to complete his dental repairs on his patients, we do whatever necessary to complete our collection goals on parent who are obligated to pay.

There was one other attorney a white male who worked in our office but I had very little contact with him because he handle a different part of the alphabet; we only talked about sports mostly, he had a treadmill in his office, and would walk while working, I must say he lost a lot of weight and he would drink all these health drinks. I would ask him questions occasionally we had a pretty good relationship, he was cool also, he was from southern California. He was a quiet guy around my age, had a few children around the same age as mine, our kids might have played against each other because they were in the same league but different high schools. He was cool guy!

I had one Mexican young lady who was funny and we really liked and enjoyed each other company, she was cool older woman who was not hung up on all the racial bullshit, she was just a couple of years older, her parents raised her well, she had a good attitude, she would ask me if I wanted to ride with her to serve clients sometimes she told me I could be her Luca Brasi from The Godfather one movie, I was her back up, she was armed and I was not, I was there to answer any questions the client may have on the spot. She use to say we are like Tom and Jerry, Peaches and Herb, Sly and Family Stone; we use too start singing " if you want to stay I be around today" and started cracking up laughing and head over to the next clients home or back to the office. We had fun driving around to different home and serving clients, while laughing every step of the way.

195

MILD ATMOSPHERE

I made sure I tried to keep the atmosphere in the office at a mild level because I do not know how many of you actually worked in an office full of women; I use to tell them the reason they cannot get alone with their husbands is because they could not get alone with each other they stayed mad at each other for some reason or another. I would have co-workers come talk to me about different issues in their lives, about other co-workers doing something to them, I would sometime talk to them about my issued I had at home sometime, at this time my home life was pretty good; but we had issue also being married and raising two young Black kids in our world today. Marriage and babies would complicate any relationship, even though finances is the first issue that would destroy your relationship or marriage. They say if a couple have a baby, get a job, get married and then move in together they have an eighty five percent chance of getting a divorce, but If the two have a job, get married, get a place of resident, then have a baby, this marriage have at least a ninety percent chance of survival, any other way the percentages of divorce will increase dramatically. People need to think about a few things before they get married and start thinking about starting a family; you want to think about are you older and mature enough for a spouse and child, if your partying days is starting to slow down or ended, you should have a stable place of employment, you know a job, and you will need a good supply of patience for your husband and your child, you will also need a good supply patience for yourself also. Being married and raising a family was the single most difficult acts I have ever complete in my life; more difficult than completing high school, college, football double session and a death in your family or any other issues in my life, because I always thought if I failed as a parent, lose my job, my home, get a divorce then what will happen to my kids, that is what scared me the most, if I end up living under a freeway or on the street so do my children, these scenario's scared the shit out of me.

SOFTBALL

I had a heavy set co-worker; she was cool and she loved playing sports, she played and liked watching it no matter what season baseball, football, basketball, I believe baseball was the game she loved most. She use to tease me because sometime I would say I'm "finna" go home or I "finna" go to lunch, she use to think it was so funny, it did not faze or bother me plus she was nice lady that like sports and did not fuck with me, I was just happy with that because at So-Low it was like walking through a minefield with disrespect and insults you never know when someone is going to say something stupid, but she was a good officer she worked with me for approximately four or five years before I retired. Next!

THOROUGHBRED

We had a health Mexican woman who black man would call her thick like a shake, we was good friends she had a good attitude, she was a single parent of two children and she was fine, healthy and like to walk around the office letting everyone know how fine she is, she like wearing nice business outfits that fit her well, she had more style then a lot of the women from the country town we worked in and she had a nice walk, her and I was pretty cool from the first time we met, she started years after I and she was about ten years younger, she had a good sense of humor she use to talk about my big head, she use to tell me my head had its own weather system; I use to tell her when she be walking down the halls and I'm walking behind her, she always make me think about the thoroughbred horses at the race track, I would tell her I always start looking for the betting booths, we use to crack up laughing and go on about our business. I kidded around and complimented all the women in the office all the time at work; even if I really did not like someone, I opened and held doors for all of them all the time because I did not want any of them mad at me, that would have been worst, once I realized and understood where I was employed and who I was employed with, I felt each and every woman could have gotten me terminated at any time, I refuse to let my guard down in the office, it did not take me long at all to come to this conclusion, really my first day on the job with the racist attorney he basically pulled the sheet off the racism and exposed the entire county of So-Low.

GIRL PLUS GIRL

We had a couple of lesbians in the office, we got alone great, they was both nice and cool women, they was not dating each other just co-workers one was Mexican and the other young lady was white, the white woman and I had a training class together off site so we set near each other even though we did not drive together, I could tell they was lesbians because they both always wore pants every day and a long button up shirt, the white woman had long hair and the Mexican woman had short hair. The white woman and I was sitting in the class and the instructor was Black woman, she had us doing a lot of role playing and this particular skit we was working on, we had to do some interacting with a straight and gay individual. This is when she realized her and I could be good friends because of how I responded to one of the question in the skit, one question was how do I feel about the gay community; I responded by saying I was always brought up to accept people for who they are, not for what I want them to be, so basically to each its own as long as the other individual did not try to pressure me into their lifestyle we would not have any problems. The white young lady had a good sense of humor and we got along well; we worked together for a long time she might have retired by now. The Mexican woman had short hair and she was brought up in a Mexican neighborhoods and earned her medals on the streets of Los Angeles; she would have been more than happy to kick your ass, we was cool, she would also kick my ass and I know she would, we would sometime look at pictures of girls together in her office, she would sometime say, Harry you should try it with another man and I would say "No Thank You"! We would crack up, she was a good friend of mine, I did not have to worry about her saying anything stupid like some of my other co-workers she was the only co-worker who boycotted the So-Low parking lot with me, we worked together for some time. I had lots a smiles and laughs with both them. We had one man who might have been gay, but who knows, he worked in the office for a very short period, he was a nice guy who was good on the computer and could type just as fast as the women in the office, typing was my weakness my finger would hit two or three keys at the same time you would hear me banging the keys in another office, I went through five keys boards in my twenty years of employment, I would type three words a minute and two of them would be misspelled, I was like a bull in the china shop on the keyboards, he was much more efficient than I was on the computer he could navigate his way through the system better than a lot of the women in the office, he could do drawings, illustrations, and make signs, I believe the women in the office started giving him a hard time, he left after a couple years of employment he took his expertise to another company and I thought he was an asset for So-Low, he respected me because I did not look down on him, the white women and some Hispanic co-workers was disrespecting him because they did not see him as a man, he was not flamboyant around the office and until this day I am still not sure which way would he go and it is also none of my business. He came by my office one day before he went to his new job he say he wanted to think me for always being cool with him, he said I never made him feel uncomfortable and he appreciated that, I told him people have been trying to look down on me and trying to make me feel uncomfortable and unequal all my life because of the color of my skin, I never like the feeling why should I make you feel that way, why would I think you would like it, he sent me a friend request and he is one of my Facebook friends now, he is just a good hearted young man who like to smile and there is nothing wrong with that and his business is his business, as long he does not try to lead me down that road, and no one really knows what road he is on. I had no problem with him. Next!

MUSTANG

We had an office manager who came after Willie retired, she was nice older woman who loved to cook and was a good cook, she would bring in all types of food dishes to work and I was eating all of them, she would bring desserts, cakes, chicken dishes and roast beef because she lives on a farm in the outskirts of the So-Low, she raised her own cattle, chickens, and also had horses. She had two sons who was never going to want for anything in life, both the sons liked me a lot, she use to tell me I should see her home, she invited me out to the farm on more than on occasion but I always had a prior engagement or I would have took her up on her offer. She want me to see her kitchen and I wanted to see it, I believe she had two of every item in her kitchen, two large ranges, two refrigerators, two dishwashers, she told me her kitchen was about three times the size of a normal large kitchen, huge walk in pantry and I believe she had a walk in freezer, I heard it was a huge log cabin style home she had a huge barn, you get the ideal like the Ponderosa minus Hop-Sing. She was married and I met her husband a couple times during the time we worked together, he was cool and she love her husband, she was nice older women who would help me when needed, she was very knowledgeable when it came to CS.

SALUTE!

We had a young man start working at the division who was fresh out of the military; most of the women was afraid of him because he walked with his back straight, eyes forward with a stone face, I believe he was a marine, the women did not like him to much at the beginning because he was questioning their decisions and the strategy they was using to get to their decision, he scared my ass also because he was a soldier he had seen combat and you never know what he had seen and what type of mental damage was done. I got to know him pretty good over time, prior to getting know him; I would hit the flood in my mind every time he walked by me, he was younger then I and after getting to know him we became pretty cool. He only had one problem that I knew of, he and another male co-worker had got into a little confrontation over a couple slices of pizza at a potluck lunch, I guess they both grab the same slice at the exact same time, they quit talking, but he was cool with me, I asked him what do you do if you have to take a shit while in combat he said you might have pee on yourself or wait, he said but he never thought about peeing in the middle of combat with your adrenaline running, he said if you smoke a cigarette it will make you have to take a shit, I tried it and it works now I have a cigarettes each day, no, I am just playing he was a good military officer, a good officer, and a good man. He asked me how did I work in this office for twenty years, I told him it was not easy, I was heavily medicated, I would sometimes smoke some weed before work when they got on my nerves to the point I thought about kicking some ones ass, I use to tell them when they go low; I get high! I told him it is a shame when you have to worry about your co-workers more than your clients, all these problems in the world and you have to worry about the people in your office doing and saying something inappropriate, he knew where I was coming from, he was a good discipline young man, a soldier, and a friend, I believe he just got married and was starting his family when I retired.

MY BUDDY

I also had another buddy I was cool with he was a lot younger and he was a fan of the football team across the bay and I was a fan of the Oakland teams because I grew up on the Oakland side of the bay, he did also, but I understood why he was a Forty-Niner fan because he grew up watching Montana and Rice when he was young, and I grew up watching the Raiders with Ken Stabler and Jack Tatum, we had a pretty good friendship, he invited me by his home and I met his wife and kids, we had a lot of laugh over time because he started working with me at a young age, we worked together for about thirteen years. He disappointed me only one time during our work history together; he witness an incident I was involved in and I told him I was going to give the State Agency who I reported the incident too his name as a witness and he got scared and told me he cannot get fired so he does not know if he was going to tell the truth or just say he did not see what happen, I told him they cannot fire him because he told the truth, he still said he not sure if he wants to do it, it puzzled me that he would not tell the true for me, all I needed him to do is be honest, I started to think maybe he had something to hide himself and he wanted no attention targeted toward him, but I had a tough time accepting him as a true friend because he wouldn't be honest for me, I decided to leave him off the witness list because I was not sure if I could trust him to tell the truth for me, we still continue to be pretty good friends but I always had this doubt about him, I even invited him over to my home a couple times and he BBQ at my party one time, we still had a lot of laughs together over time, I believe he slipped up and told me one day why he did not want any attention targeted toward him years later and just to let you know what type of friend I am, I will respect him and keep it to myself. At the end of our employment together I still until this day consider him a pretty good friend of mine, we talked a lot of shit together and had a lot of laughs.

COSTA RICA

We had another young man who transferred to So-Low from another division of the county; he was already with the county and came from another division, he was cool he had the opportunity to climb the letter pretty fast because he had a degree; he was sports oriented so he fit in the office pretty well with all the other fellas, he would sometime running the betting pools and kept track of the money and the scores. I also had a good friend from Costa Rica who worked in the accounting department; he would always help me with the accounting portion of my case we also had a lot of laughs during our years of working together, he wanted me and my wife to travel to Costa Rica with him and his wife because he had a lot of family still in Costa Rica, he stated we would have a good time, I told him my wife is not going to Costa Rica where you might see a monkeys running free along with all the other inhabitants animals and insects, he said the beaches, trails, water and falls are fantastic, the scenery is as beautiful as a person can see, he also said the scenery from different areas of the country is beautiful day, night or at sun down, he said it is like no other place in the world. He showed me many pictures of his country because he and his wife would travel to their home land every few years; I believe he use to tell me a lot of people think Costa Rica is an island but it is not, it the body of land in Central America that connects North America and South America he said his country is beautiful, I told him if I ever get enough money together I would travel down there with him he ended up getting a new job and moving on to bigger and better things, I would always consider him a good young man and friend.

I also met this white young lady she was a nice looking but she was mean. When I first met her; I did not know if she was just a racist or just plain old mean. I am smiling while writing about her; she was in love with this one guy; he did not work with us; he worked or owned a bar in town my co-workers and I went to the bar the one night. This was the only night I stayed in town until one thirty in the morning and the police followed me out of town; it was a good the freeway entrance was just a few blocks up or I am sure they would have pulled me over. She loved him; she had three kids by him and they are doing well; but when she was pregnant with those three different babies I use to ask her how she was doing; if she needed anything every day; she finally started to smile. I watched all three kids grow to the age of ten, eight and six years old; she would tell you exactly how she feel; I had watered her down and I do not believe she was a racist she just acted mean and tough; but she was just a nice woman deep down inside. I had her all broke down by the time I retired, I would be surprised if she did not call me a friend, but you never know!

I worked with this short nice young Mexican woman who was married and had five kids with her husband; she was working every day; handled her kids and did everything for her family, the only thing I did not like about her; whenever we was in meetings and management was bring the meeting to an end; management would asked does anyone have any questions; she always had at least four or five more questions while everyone else was trying to get back to their offices; she continued asking questions, they were all intelligent questions, whenever management asked is there any questions; it was guarantee she would be the employee who will ask another question or four. One time before the end of the meeting; I leaned over to her and whispered in her ear, do not ask any questions at the end of the meeting, I have something to do; she looked at me and she whispered back in my ear, shut up Harry, I don't care what you have to do, before I kick your ass, we cracked up and when management asked does anyone have any questions; she raised her hand and asked at least three questions while looking at me. I would have kicked her ass; but she was shorter than me. Next!

A GOOD YOUNG LADY

There was a young lady who was not a racist; she was smart but every man who entered her life has let her down her father passed at a young age suddenly; she was raised by her mother and her older sisters; she was smart and pretty, I had a little spot in my heart for her, she use to call me her Homey! She really loved her father, her boyfriend took advantage of her good heart in her early twenties caused her some financial issues which she was able to eventually overcome in time; by working hard every day, but what woman have not been taking advantage of by a man at one time or another in their lives. I had the upmost respect for her and we had many discussions concerning her situations; I am glad she was able to pull through her adversity and come out shining like a diamond. We had a lot of laughs together through the years we worked together; I watch her grow from a young lady to a mature woman. Before I retired I told her to keep on pushing with her life, and she will meet a good man someday. Next!

OH NO!

I had this female co-worker called my office and asked me to come to her office, so I stopped what I was doing and walked to her office she asked me to examine the case on her computer screen, as I was examining the case; I notice the father on the case had the same last name as the female officer; I said he has the same last name as you, I said is he your brother, but she had never mention a brother to me in all the conversations we had together; she said that is my husband; I said no he's not; she yes he is; I said do you know the mother; she said yes, he introduced her to me; he introduced her to me as a friend, the child on the case was older than the child they had together; she was hurt behind this information she discovered. I left out of the office and she called her husband and lit in to his ass, she was crying and cursing him out in Spanish, he was starting to have health problems; she told him to get out today. I felt bad for her because she was a nice young lady trying to raise her child; now she has to raise the child as a single parent; I told her she is in the right place to open up a case and he will have to pay, she told me she did not know how she was going to raise her child; I told her she is going to keep on pushing with her life and her child's life; I also told her she is not the only single parent out there, I offered her some encouragement and told her she can do it. She was lacking in self-esteem because she had a weight issue while in her teens; she woke up one day and when to work on herself; now she is a very beautiful woman and enjoy working on her appearance; she became an exercise alcoholic, she stayed at the gym or exercise at home. I told her she has bedroom eyes, eyes green, brown skin, weight one thirty five, she literally transform her body, she also has a good kid. Next!

DON'T DO IT

I also had a coworker who was a lot of fun at the beginning we had a lot of laughs; she had a child when I met her, a bi-racial child they was cool, I enjoy talking to her son from time to time. All of a sudden she met this Black young man who I thought was to demanding and selfish; he wanted her to change her way of thinking even when it came down to her favorite sports team; she had to started rooting for his team. She did not like changing her way of thinking to his, I told her one day; what if he is an idiot, you do not want to follow an idiot. I did not like him for those reasons and other things he said to her; she was always upset, her behavior and attitude suffered; she ended up having a couple more children over the next five years before she left him. She is a strong lady when she think for herself and now that she is no longer with him she will have plenty of time to think for herself; I am glad for her, because she has a lot potential and she did not need some knucklehead trying to run her life. Next!

RETIREMENT IS NEAR

Retirement was starting to cross my mind a little more often going into my nineteenth year; I could not believe I made it this far without killing someone in the office; or at least beating someone down; this thought has cross mind on a daily bases between home life and work life it was starting to take its toll on me. I was starting to loss my smile; people that know me; know I am a reasonably happy guy, any person that met me in the office know I have a since of humor that is my way of making through life without losing my mind; I feel you must laugh to neutralize the stress life will bring on a person.

Approximately April of twenty eighteen I was in at meeting with our lead counsel after our discussion, I was exiting his office and ran into our office manager's; she was in her office so I stepped in and said hi, we started small talking and while talking; I realized my name was on her computer; I asked her what is my name doing on her computer and she said she is working on the budget for the CSD. She had me due to retire in twenty-twenty two; I told her I cannot do another four years in here. Our office manager knew I had been through some rough times in the office; she worked with me for at least fifteen years at this time, I told her I plan to do twenty years and I will be getting the hell out of here. She then stated I might want to leave at the end of twenty-eighteen because if I leave after the end of this years which was my twentieth year, our life time medical payout was going to be lower from six hundred and fifty dollars a month to four hundred a month, this payout was promised to each and every employee. That really got me thinking about retiring; I was not going to take another pay cut on this job; because our union representative agree to have our life time medical payout decreased by two hundred and fifty dollars. I called my union representative and asked him why he agreed to take a pay cut on our medical payout, he fed me some dog shit that turned into bullshit about he thought it was our best move; I told him; he do not know what is best for me and all the other employees without talking to us first. He said he is doing the best job he can, I told him do not do your best for me again especially when you are taking money out of the employee's pockets. I told my office manager I will talk it over with my wife and family; I will get back to her with my decision, I went home and did not mention retiring to my wife that day because I wanted to think about the entire situation myself before bring it to my wife's attention; I like to think things out before I make a decision on what is the best move for me and my family. After talking to a few more co-workers about the retirement process I was getting closer and closer to leaving the CSD after all I did not like working there and really never have like working there. So I started asking management about the medical payout that we was promised; the six hundred and fifty dollars a month for the remainder of my life and I ask the office manager could I get the six fifty a monthly payout in cash, check or auto deposit and everyone I spoke to stated I should be able to receive the payout each month on top of my PERS retirement, I was thinking I should be alright with the money I will be receiving, then when I turn sixty-two; I will get my social security, I was going to turn fifty-nine six months after I retire. I was feeling good about my game plan for retirement instead of me getting on my wife's medical plan; I can take the six fifty and get on Obama Care and also pay for my daughter's medical coverage who is under the age of twenty six, I could use the remainder of money to cover some of my bills. My wife is working so we can actually make this happen and I will still be living pretty comfortable. I started to smile a little more at this time because I knew

I had made twenty years and I was in a position to retire and get the hell out of this office. I spoke to my wife about retirement she was happy for me because she could since the change in my behavior from all the stress I was receiving on the job from my clients and co-workers, she knew all these problems was starting to weigh heavy on my heart; we set down and weighed out the pros and cons of me retiring. I returned to the office and told our office manager I was going to retire; she told me I have to contact the administration office retirement division and set up a meeting with our retirement representatives and they will go over the steps needed to complete my retirement. I contact So-Low retirement division and spoke to a Mexican retirement representative her name was Maria she told me to wait until later in the year for my meeting to be completed; she told me meetings are usually about ninety days prior to my retirement date; she set my retirement interview for September of twenty eighteen, I had to retire by the end of the year so I set my retirement date December Twenty Eighth of twenty eighteen. I was walking around the office like I finally made through all this bullshit in this office. I had some co-workers who was happy for me like, this white young lady I had worked with for about ten years she was a pretty and fine young lady who live at home with her parents and her three kids she needed help raising; I believe all her kids was all by the same father and she had them at a young age, their father started having health problems at a young age and it made things really difficult for her to work and raise three young kids; I believe she had two girls and a boy, the boy was born in the middle, I got to know all three kids they was nice kids, the girls was nice young ladies approximate ages was fourteen and ten years old, the boy was about twelve years old at the time. I spoke to her son about sports and gave him a few pointers about football, baseball, and basketball, because he would sometime come by my office and talk to me while waiting for his mother to finish work; I told him he should play all three sports because it will make him an all-around better athlete and he would develop all his muscle instead of just certain muscles, different sports use different muscles I even drove out and saw a couple of his games, I taught him the three ways of catching a baseball when it is hit to him, I told him if the ball is hit below his waist have his glove pointed downward; if the ball is hit between his waist to his head turn his glove sideways and catch the ball and if the ball is hit or thrown above his head then turn the glove upward; that was the way I was taught to catch a ball at a young age. I really liked their mother not only was she fine she was a good mother and a nice young lady; a good friend, she ended up transferring to a another county after I retired she told me she never like or agreed with the way I was treated but she could not saying anything on my behalf; she was never in position to say anything, we had a lot of laughs together over the years she also had a good sense of humor. Next!

Get out the way!

Another co-worker who always treated me with respect was a middle aged white woman; she was married and had a mentally handicapped daughter who I loved; she was approximately ten years of age when we first met I believe she had down syndrome but she was my friend. I used to tell her mother; I would be on the elevator and her daughter would be on the ground level waiting to get on the elevator; when the elevator doors opened up, instead of her waiting for me to get off; she would push me out the way while we are both walking through the doors. I would tell her mother she would push me out of the way "like get your ass out of my way!" we would crack up, she would wave at me from her bus when she got picked up for school each morning in front of the job; I would be arriving to work every morning at about the time the bus would pick her daughter up. Her mother would straighten me or anyone else out if she had too concerning her daughter, she loved her daughter too no end and she was not going to let anyone or anything hurt her daughter, neither was I. She was a good mother and a nice lady and she had a good husband who loved his daughter. Next!

BIG KID

I had a white female co-worker and single mother, she had a child with a man and they produce a son who was bigger than most of the people in the office, her son was about ten years old at the time I met him, he was about five feet ten inches tall, at the beginning the father of her son did not want to have anything to do with them. But I believe eventually the son did have an opportunity to develop a relationship with his father. His mother and father continue to have issues in their relationship which cause them not to reunite, she was a nice young lady who was struggling to survive with her kid because the father was not always handling his financial responsibility, nor was he handling his parental obligation. Her son was acting out to the point it was hard for her to control him, he was just bad, he was bigger than the average kids his age. She would ask me to talk to him, I was telling him he need to be cool; I told him his mother is the only person he had in his life who really cared for him and he does not want to lose her and if he is going to be nice to anyone, it should be his mother. He would sit up and listen to what I was telling him like I was the first Black person he had a conversation with, and I am sure I was the first Black person he had a conversation with, but he listen to what I was telling him and started acting better toward his mother. I believe they have a good and loving relationship now because he started growing up and maturing as a young man; he should be about twenty years old now, with these young kids today, you just have to be glad they do not do anything stupid that can potentially ruin their lives. I am sure he is still one of the biggest kids around last time I saw him he was starting to look like a big offensive tackle, I am sure he is doing well, I hope! Let's move on.

SANDWICH

They built a Subway Sandwich restaurant down the street from my office. I never really eat at subways; only when I get into one of my health frame of mind stages, I would go to subways and get a sandwich. One day I decided to get a sandwich, it was a pretty long line, I was about six customers deep, I was standing behind this middle age white woman, she was about fifty years of age, she was dressed in business attire, there was a couple of students standing in front of her; as the line moved forward there was some high schools students in line behind me and the woman. All of sudden this young man walked in and was slapping five with all the students behind me like he was Mr. Cool, then he seen the students standing in front of us, so he walked to the students that was standing in front of us, he looked back at me like he was intimidating me, the kids in front me placed their order, the young man started to try to place his order, I told him you not next, get your ass to the back of the line, the white woman moved to the side, I looked at the Mexican young man and he looked at me, I told him to get to the end of the line, he looked at me as he started to walk to the back of the line and said you better watch you back, and I looked at him and told him you better watch your front. The white woman said thanks a lot, what a fucking ass; I told her no problem, he is nothing but a little asshole, growing up to be a full grown asshole, and will take an ass whooping because he is a asshole and assholes always eventually take an ass whooping. She waited for me to get my sandwich and walked out with me, while we was walking by the young Mexican boy, I stopped and turned my back to him and his friends, then I turned back around and looked at him and told him you need to be cool before someone

219

fuck you up, I told him pain does not feel good, you might want cool out. The white woman told me thanks again outside while she was getting in her car to go back to work, that was the last time I saw her or the young man. Next!

PLEASE LET ME HELP YOU

Approximately two months prior to my retirement I was exiting the building to go home for the evening; I saw one of my co workers park in her truck in front of the CSD. She is a pretty blond headed woman who was a very good officer, she was intelligent, sufficient, and learn things fast and communicated with the clients well. I always thought she was a good officer, she had worked there for approximately three years. She was parked in front of the office with her window down and listening to music, I walked over and said hi to her, when she said hi backed to me, she slurred her language and I said are you alright, she said yeah Harry, I am fine, I said you been drinking and I looked in her car and saw a half empty bottle of Vodka on the passenger seat, she said I had a package mailed to the office and I have to go in and get it. I asked her if she wants me to get it, she said no I will get it, she tried to get out of her truck, but started falling out of her truck, I caught her and told her I will get her package. I walked in to the lobby of the CSO and told the receptionist that I was picking up Kerri's package, the receptionist could see Kerri in her truck from the receptionist desk through the windows. I took the package back out to her and told her she is not in any condition to drive, she kept insisting that she was ok, I offered to drive her home, she said no, I told her to let me rent a room for her to sober up in, she said no, she is alright, I said please do not drive she said Harry I will be fine. I thought about taking her car keys, but I did not want to make scene, because if the cops came they might shot me in my ass, I said Kerri please be careful, I worried about that woman all night, I even told my wife about the incident, when I got to work the next morning and she was not at work. About an hour later,

I heard she was pulled over and received a DUI about five blocks from the job, her and her husband had a big fight and she went out and had some drinks. This was a mother of four kids, good kids because she asked me to talk to her son about wearing protection while having sex. I am happy to say that she cleaned up her act and is doing fine now, her kids is happy, she did lose her job because of the DUI, she went to rehab and she is clean and doing fine, I am happy to say, and her son listened to what I told him about wearing protection! God is good!

RETIREMENT MEETING

In September we met for my retirement meeting, the meeting last for about an hour, the meeting was conducted by Maria and this blond headed woman name Kim they gave me their retirement spill, and asked me if I had any questions for them, I told them I had one questions and one question only. I said this question has to do with the six hundred and fifty dollars a month medical payout the So-Low and our union negotiated and I was promised to receive; they said yes what question, I asked did the medical payout get mailed to Kaiser or to me? They said it can be mail where ever I wanted it mailed, I said so I can have it mailed to me each month for the rest of my life six hundred and fifty dollar, they both responded yes, I asked when would I start receiving it, they stated around 1/5/2019 for the first check, then it should be deposited by the first of each month from that point on, I said great, do I need to sign anything; no we have your bank account number already, it will be auto deposited each month in your account. I asked them are you sure everything is going to work out this way, and they said yes. I told both ladies this six hundred and fifty dollars is the reason I am retiring, I told them it is due to go down to four hundred at the end of this year, I told them it cannot go wrong . I left the administrated building and drove back to the CSD and when in my office, set at my desk and call my union representative, he answer my call I told him I was considering retiring, he said great, I told him I am retiring because the six hundred fifty dollars medical payout that you negotiated to four hundred a month, I said you sure you are on our side you should never give up any progress, I told him he was going backwards, he was glad to be getting rid me because he had made other moves that I did think

223

was too smart and I pointed them out to him. He said Harry you are one of our union member that carried the medical coverage for your entire family, I said yes, I carried the medical for my entire family, he said well you are not suppose receive six fifty, you should receive twelve fifty five a month, because you took care of your entire family, I said the retirement representative never mention this to me, I said you sure, he said yes, he sent me a two line email with the MOU code stating this fact, I called Maria again and verified that I was suppose receive this amount, she said yes that is true. I told her I am retiring for sure, with my PERS retirement and this extra twelve fifty five coming in, I should be alright. I was feeling good, I told myself I will talk everything over with my wife tonight, and start to get out of this racist ass office. Because deep down inside I hated going to work out there I never knew when I would be called a nigger; I never knew when I would walk in the men's restroom and see the pervert central show, I never knew when I was going to be disrespected again. I am not a violent person but my horoscope sign is Gemini so I have a good side and a bad side, I try to stay on the happy-go-lucky side of my personality but every once in a while someone would make me introduce the bad side of me to them, this is something I do not like doing but when necessary I will, plus now a days they take you to jail for fighting. Back when I was younger you can take a person to fight club and did not have to worry about catching case and doing jail time. Work became a lot less stressful after I spoke to wife about retiring from So-Low, my wife was not too surprise because every time something happen to me at work she heard about it that evening, she knew I was have a difficult time dealing with all the crap coming my way. She told me to quit and started looking for another place to work, but I had started accumulating a little time on the job, I was older, I knew if I went somewhere else I would have to start all over, and what if my next supervisor and mangers was worst then what I had now, that may be hard to believe that my management could be worst then what I had. I started thinking I am finally getting rid of these motherfucker's in about three months. I continued to do my job for the next few months and as I got closer to my retirement date 12/28/2018, I started using some of my sick leave because I was not going to be compensated for my sick leave just my vacation day, I had a lot of vacation days accrued at least three weeks of vacation, I used all my sick leave during the my last three months.

All my coworkers was happy and sad to see me retiring; they all seen what I was going through, some was happy I did not have to continue go through the shit I had gone through, some was sad to see me go because they knew when I left the excitement in the office was going with me, they knew I was the entertainment and if there was any laughter going on in the office I was going to be somewhere in the vicinity. Everyone was telling me they was sad to see me go, some said they was jealousy of me because I was leaving, all I knew was this ride was coming to an end and there was no one happier then I was, if this job was an amusement park ride, I was becoming sick to my stomach at this time of my employment with So-Low. There was some of my co-workers who I will miss, some who had disrespected me in the pass, I looked at them like I taught them something about treating not only the Blacks but all people of color they may encounter in their future travels through life. You know the hardest words in the Lord's prayers is "forgive our trespassers as we forgive those who trespass against us". When somebody cross you in a negative way, it is hard to forgive the person who disrespected you, well it is the same with me, I have a very difficult time forgiving the person, but since the Bible states this fact and I have been saying my prayers since I learned my prayers at the age of five every night, I find a way to forgive them one way or another, some may take you a little longer to forgive. Well I found a way to forgive a few of the co-workers depending on what they have done to me. Some of my coworker have not been forgiven and I been retired for four years now.

Let get back to my retirement: The office decided they wanted to throw the retirees a party and they wanted me to invite my family. They always had a pot luck style lunch, my sisters asked me was they going to cater the lunch, I said no pot luck style lunch, they say you kidding and started laughing, I told them these are country fried people, their formal wear is jeans and plaid collared shirts. I been working there for twenty years and no one but one of my nieces came to the office and that is because she live a little north of So-Low, my kids came once or twice to the office, but I really did not want them to come to the office half the time, so why would I bring in family, plus all my family lived in the bay area which was a hour and a half drive for them. My co-workers was driving me crazy about inviting my family to my party, we had couple other ladies that retired on the same day as I. I told my wife about the retirement lunch and she said she would come if I wanted her too. I knew when I told my family they would come, because I am the baby of the family and we all have a close relationship with each other, I had been to their retirement parties. I have four brothers and two sisters and I am the youngest, and I LOVE IT. Well just like I said my two sisters came with my wife and one brother all attended my retirement party, they met all the characters you have heard about and they knew about every incident I had been through. I had an opportunity to address the retirement party; the first thing I told my co-workers; I feel like I just finished a game of "Jumanji", I cannot believe I actually made through So-Low, I feel like I just got a fat lady in leather pants off my back. I told them I love each and every one of them, some more than others, but I am so glad this is over and I can sit down I never thought this day would come. I know I told my co-workers over the past years if I had

226

a chance to retire I would not do it because I love the kids of So-Low; now that I have reached the retirement stage; I am Gone! I am out of here! Later! Fuck the kids of So-Low! My co-workers would look at me and we all cracked up, and they would say Harry you are crazy. I left early from work the day of my retirement party since my family was all there, I showed them my office and the cubicle they had me housed in. We went back to my home and set around the house for a couple of hours and talk about my accomplishment and how I survived this job. There was no one more excited than I was about my retirement. I almost cried a couple times because I was so happy to be out of there, I felt like a civil rights leader after I walked out of there because I had a dream that all white people in the office would learn from me how to respect other people of color, I went through a modern day lynching, I had never been treated and belittled this bad in an office environment in my life. I worked for companies like Bank of America, Citibank, Citicorp Savings, Legal collection agency, and a Law firm at Jack London Square in the city of Oakland. This is a perfect example of systemic racism in the work place and the only way to defeat it is to try your best to promote people not because of the color of their skin, but the content of their character and who is going to be as fair as possible, you must have diversity because diversity breeds diversity, and the people who is in charge now cannot have racial bias hang ups, the black woman you may promote might just be the best person for the job, and he or she may be the best person you ever promoted, that same person may promote you one day because you showed trust in them at one time. You cannot stop an employee from going on one side of the building because this person asked another employee how she is doing, I do not care if the person is handicapped or not. You do not sit a cubicle etiquette paper in a co-workers seat to antagonize one of your employees to the point they do not want to work for you, let along look at you. You do not punish people because of the car they drive and you do not have the director of the division standing in the restroom with his drawls on his ankles so everyone could see his junk. I asked myself am I wrong? I keep coming up with a no answer. You do not tell your employee that is too much information when they come report a negative incident about another employee or management, you handle the problem and you take the necessary step to rectify the problem. When you have people like this in management you have a recipe for disaster and that is exactly what this office was a disaster. If management was rated by stars I would give them no stars for the treatment I received during the course of my employment. You can call me a disgruntle employee and I will tell you to go through the shit I have gone through and see how you like it. I never trusted So-Low because they never gave me any reason to trust them; I had to just wait to see if they was going to do me right about by my retirement and my medical payout.

Here is one more reason you can be disgruntle; after I retire I was at home and I received my first retirement check from PERS, it was the correct amount minus taxes. So-Low had the medical payout issued from an insurance company called BPPI insurance which was located in northern California; the check I received was a thousand dollars short, I called the retirement representative Maria and asked her what the hell is going on? She apologize and told me she would get it corrected, I was pissed I told her do not fuck with my money! She said she will get it corrected immediately, I received this check in early January, on February the first I receive another check this one was short about nine hundred dollars, I called Maria and I told her the check was short again and she tried to apologize again, and I told her I did not want to hear this shit, I want her to get my money straighten out, I asked her to have her superior call me if she cannot get my money straighten out and send me the money that they agreed to give me. So she had another check cut to for about six hundred and fifty which I received before the end of February, close but no cigar, I called Maria and she told me she wanted me to talk to Helen her boss. You may remember Helen she was the administrated representative I spoke with when So-Low suspended me for two weeks without pay because I drove my Mercedes Benz to work. She was the women who refuse to take three or four hundred out of each of my pay checks until I paid back the two week. She's the woman who told me it would not be a punishment without taking my entire check, she was the woman that did not give a damn about my family. I spoke to her on the phone and she told me since they are not sending me the correct amount she is going to stop my medical payout all together and hung up the phone. I called her back and she let it go to voice mail, I called Maria back and she did not answer this went on for days. This action did not surprise me at all. So-Low was cheating me because they never treated their minority employees with respect. Helen called BPPI insurance company and had the medical payout stopped all together. I called Helen another day and I told her exactly what I thought of her sorry ass, I told her she was a low down cheat for stopping my money, and not correcting the issue, I also told her she was not going to get away with this shit, she try to tell me I said I did not want the medical payout, I told her do she know any person that does not want their money and I told her to show it to me in writing where I said I did not want my money, she couldn't because it did not exist.

I called my union representative James and told him Maria never got my medical payout money straighten out and Helen has cut off the payout all together. He played like he did not remember tell me I was to receive the twelve hundred and fifty five a month. I told James if you was standing in front of me right now I would kick his lien ass. I worked the last twenty years of my life and contributed money to a piece of shit ass Union and So-Low. I did not go talk to them in person because I was very upset and I did not want to do anything that was going to get me incarcerated. This redneck county would have been more than happy to have me incarcerated and would have given me as much time as they could have sentence me, or else I would have went up to the office and stuck my foot all up in their asses. You do not treat people like I was treated, and I am sure there is a lot more people being treated like me in the United States work force across the country and it need to be investigated and stopped immediately. This is not surprising they treated me like they did. I remember So-Low cheated this Mexican young lady out of her design she created on her office system. She created this program on how to track her cases and (Pervert Central) like the program and he took it to the state of California and the state is still using her program today, they never gave her the credit for her design, no money or the patent rights she deserved. They just stole her design; just like they been stealing my money for the last four years. I called BPPI Insurance company which is the company I received the checks in the wrong amount and spoke to an female representative name Julie, she asked for the last four digits of my social security number and my account came right up, she told me the only reason my money is not being sent to me is because Helen from So-Low stopped all monthly allotment payments. This is a perfect example why the public is going into work places and shooting up places of employment, hell I thought about it, for a minute, I am not going to lie, but I am not going to prison for anyone but my family. I told myself I believe in the Lord; I will let him handle it, he see their ugliness and I am sure he will fix my issue in his time. In his time, it will bring me my back pay and I will want my back pay.

That is about the time I set down and started writing this book to let the world know that systemic racism is running rapid in this country, it is in every nook and cranny of the nation, and where ever there are white people. I have some great white friends that I care about, but it's the assholes who fuck the world up. All nationalities have assholes, but some nationalities have a few more asshole then others, you never know who the asshole is until they say something stupid and look into a mirror. To cheat a fellow employee is against the law in some areas in the state, but in So-Low you have white privilege on top of white privilege, and it needs to stop, I would not be surprised if Helen is receiving my money each month. I will continue to pursue my money because like the old Civil Rights Movements, Bus Boycotts and the current Black Lives Matter freedom marches in our country we will not stop until there is equal justice for all and for all means me! So do not think this fight is over, because it is not over, until it over, that mean it will not be over until I have my money in my hands. I am sure Helen and So-Low is hoping I die soon, because then they would not have to pay me my money, I want my money and if I pass away, my family want my back pay. I heard through the grapevine that we have another union representative handling So-Low area hopefully after I contact the new representative and maybe he or she can get this all straighten out and I can received the money I earned and deserve then I can get on with my life. I also heard Helen left the county for some reason, probably because she did not want to get caught stealing my money, I do not know why she left or if for sure she did leave, but it is good that she is gone because you cannot have people in management that has a negative and lousy attitude. If a company's management has a negative attitude then this company will not get the maximum effort out of their employees.

I believe I helped over one hundred thousand children during my twenty years of employment with So-Low. I did not have issues with the parents because I was married myself and I know how difficult it is in a marriage, divorce and separation happens on a daily bases for numerous reason, I also knew how difficult it was to raise kids in this world today, I did not care if you were married, not married, or your baby was conceived in the back seat of a car or in the frozen food department at Safeway's, if the DNA test came back you are the father then you are going to have to pay for that child or children. I use to tell the non-custodial parents if I am broke raising my kids; I will not be the only broke person at the party, so they will have to pay their support. They would cuss me out, threaten me, some might even try to take it out on the other parent but I would tell them there are two ways to get out of paying child support, they can move to Iraq or die, there is no other way to exit this obligation.

There is one way you can eased your pain from paying child support and that is smoke some weed. It help me deal with all the assholes I dealt with during the course of my career, shit I had to do something that was going to stop me from turning violent toward the public and my coworkers. Marijuana was a way I dealt with all the adversity and mistreatment So-Low sent my way. I never smoked it while at work, I only took a hit before and after work to calm my nerves, it was a necessity, if I was hooked then So-Low was the main reason I started smoking, the public also added to my stress listening to everyone's problems on a daily bases and the stress of marriage and raising my family all took toll on me. I did not smoke a lot until I started dealing with their bullshit, I had never been employed with a company who treated their employees so negative and unfair. By the time I retired I was smoking marijuana on a daily bases, I also worked out three to four times a week at the gym, and worked out hard, but it still was not enough to relieve the stress So-Low willingly and purposely applied to my life. I got tired of being mistreated and belittled by management and watching them mistreated the Mexican employee who was employed there with me, just because the Mexican employees would not stick together still does not justify So-Low's behavior, it was unfair and cruel.

I was not offered a legitimate opportunity to interview for a supervisor position until Rhonda asked me one day to consider interviewing for a supervisor position which had just came available and I turned her down; that is when I told her all I wanted was peace of mind at this point time in my career, I was going into my eighteenth year of employment with So-Low. I was good enough to represent them in court, but not in management by the time Rhonda asked me, my management aspirations had left the station years ago, it had dissolved like Alka-Seltzer Plus tab in a glass of water, just bubbles and dust at the bottom of the glass. I had made my decision not to interview for a supervisor position years prior to our conversation, I had more account receivable experience then every one of my co-workers, I held the subrogation manager position at the law firm I left for So-Low; Rhonda like me so much because she knew I was not afraid to voice my opinion; like when she decided to have all the bullet proof glass taken out of our interviewing booths. I went to her office and asked her was she crazy, I told her I think she is making a huge mistake with all the shooting going on in this world, I am sure there is someone out there who would not have a problem shooting up a child support office, hell they was shooting up elementary schools at this time. I told her she was opening up the state and county to a huge lawsuit. I also told her she is not protecting her employees, she said she want us to build a relationship with our clients, I said how much of relationship she want us to build with our clients we are already in their lives, and homes; she stated she still does not believe we can build a relationship with bullet proof glass between us. The only problem is she was never going down to service the clients, it was the officer's lives that was in danger every time we had a walk in. You never know who is going to be the next person to walk through those doors and what type of issues this person has in their lives, he or she could have issues in their home life, military, prison you never know. Rhonda is a nice woman and have good intentions but I still do not agree with her when it come to the bullet proof glass being removed. I hope and pray that some knucklehead or idiot does not come in and shoot up a CS office or any other place of employment one day. But all employers is obligated to do everything possible to keep their employee safe and in a clean environment. I did not think she was up holding her end of the bargain when it came to our safety and every time I walked down to assisted a client I would say a prayer to the Lord to not let this next walk in be a psycho and do something stupid that will ruin a lot of family's lives.

Let me get out of this part of my life, this is a part of my life that every time I reminisce about it make me upset because of all the mistreatment and belittlement I endured during my employment. It is a shame that any person on God's green earth would have to endure this type of treatment and belittlement while trying to raise his family and help numerous other family's across this nation we call home. I know what I have gone through is nothing like my ancestors in the nineteen sixties and earlier because they was being lynched and brutalized. What I was subjected to was the modern day lynching without the noose, water hoses, and police dogs and batons but the beatings was still just as painful and humiliating to the person that is receiving it. This person happen to be me that was taking this ass whooping and it took every ounce of my man hood not to lose my cool. There was a lot of times I had to step out of the building to stop from fucking someone up. I had this wise older black women tell me white people are truly afraid of black people, she said we scare the shit out of them, white people are afraid that black people may turn out more intelligent, that is why black schools facilities are not as good as white schools, afraid blacks may be their boss one day, that is why we are not promoted, blacks may end up superior to them in one way or another. She also said they started

234

all this shit with their prejudice ways, their lack of respect for other nationalities, and the rude behavior toward other races in the country. She said their lack of respect is the reason they are going to lose the race; the race to equality, they are going to lose because we will overcome all prejudices and lack of respect they want to issue out. We will keep on pushing, fighting and scratching for everything we deserve and that is equality and equal justice for all people of color. Black people have been withstanding the brutality but white people has been taking the ass whooping, because all the peaceful marches, the bus boycotts, the NBA not playing games, camera being worn by police and the brutality is being filmed on a daily bases, which bring the undisputed truth to the surface, to the point you cannot turn a blind eye to the truth, it is looking directly at you and all you have to do is call it like you see it. You are looking at the truth and it is setting every nationality free. White officers are being arrested and prosecuted for kneeling down on a Black man neck until he is pleading and yelling those now famous words; "I can't breathe" for nine minutes and twenty nine seconds and calling for his Momma! We are not totally there yet, matter of fact we still have a long ways to go, because they can still shoot us while we are asleep in our own beds, and shoot us in the back while being detained on a platform while exiting the Bart Train Station, or watch us bleeds out on national TV, while our fiancée is crying and filming the incident and his baby is crying for his father not to die, or being shot in back four time while walking back to your own car. These injustices has been going on since the ships sailed into ports four hundred for years ago. Just imagine all the altered police reports against people of color before cameras became mandatory, all the lies the police wrote down on their reports and society just except their explanation with no questions, if you did not have an eye witness then you did not have a chance, especially a person color. A white female co-worker ask me one day what would I do if I received my forty acres and a mule. I told her I would build me a home on my forty acres and I would use the mule to move my furniture in my home. I told her it was none of her business what I would do with my forth acres, give it to me and find out what I would do.

I know the pain I endured is not as bad as what my ancestors received but unfair treatment hurts just the same, systemic behavior in the workplace hurt just same, it hurts your self-esteem, it hurts your work habits and it hurts your motivation, and most of all it hurts your pocket book which leads back to your family. Systemic racism in the work place is designed to keep people of color in their place just like slavery, policing and political injustice, the place this particular individual believe you should be in, but who place this person in charge of your life, he or she is not the Lord Jesus Christ, last I heard God is the only person in charge of someone life, your managers job is to treat the county employees fairly and to make sure all necessary work is completed correctly and according to the company rules and regulations, not to fine fault and treat people as they see fit. This is when people start to run a stray and started treating people their sick and racist ways they learned while growing up, they forget this person is a human being and have the same goals in life to raise their children in to good law abiding citizens.

That is why diversity is important in the workplace, with diversity in the workplace it lets other nationalities see a strong intelligent male or female managerial mates. Once you see and work around another people of color and see they are capable of doing a good or better job then you. So-Low needs diversity like a hot dog need mustard, catsup, and relishes, right now So-Low has just the dry ass hot dog and the dry ass bun that their employees has to choke down. The state needs to go into So-Low and check on their hiring practices and promoting practices because in this county if you are not white, then you are not right and that is not right. Like I said before right is right rather you like it or not!

I hope you did not enjoy my agony too much, because I did not enjoy it at all, but I survived it and that is what is important. I have been lied too, cheated, misused, and belittled and I am still standing. I just wrote this because I wanted the world to hear my journey, and to let people know we may have made progress but we still have a long ways to go. So keep on trucking and keep diversity alive! Get those racist thoughts out of your mind. Love and respect each other, try it you might like it.

Now I am going to walk through my big ass house with my Mercedes Benz in the garage and put my swimming trunks on and go dive in my big ass eight foot pool. If that does not make them mad, I don't know what will! They did not help me get everything I have accrued in my life, hard work by my wife and I gave us what we have accrued in our lives and not taking no for an answer. They kept stressing me and the Lord kept blessing me! I have a big ass smile on my face right about now! One love to all the people that is experiencing systemic racism in their place of employment today, keep your head up and do not let them brake you mentally or physically, stand strong, and remember say it loud, I am black proud! Black Lives Matter! PS: I will continue to pursue my medical payout and my now four years back pay! Later!

The End!

PS: Bonus issue titled (The Elevator)

This incident happen around the time I was dealing with Pervert Central standing in the restroom with his junk out so any and everybody can see him.

This was a very hot day in So-Low, it had to be at least 105-110 degrees every home was running their air conditions and the electrical grid was being compromised. I got on the elevator and was going from the second floor to the first floor, after the doors closed and the elevator started to go down to the first floor, the elevator suddenly stopped and the lights went off. I said all shit!! So while I was standing in the dark, I had to take a piss all of sudden, so I took a piss in the corner of the elevator. Now the piss smelled and the heat in the elevator started fucking with me, and some co-worker heard me yelling that I am stuck in the elevator. While I was in the elevator more and more co-workers had gather around, I was telling them it is hot in here and I need them to get the fire department over here to open the door so I can get some air. My co-workers and managements was laughing and said they call the fire department, but I had to get my ass out of there because I was running out air, I was sweating profusely and it was no way I was going to continue to stay in the elevator, so I started to examine the door in the dark, I started feeling on the doors. The inside doors slide from left to right, it would slide one door half way and another door will continue to slide to the other slide of the elevator. I walked up to the door that close the elevator on the right hand side, and I pressed my hand on the door and was able to get the door to open enough to get my fingers in the door where I could pull it open and slide it back all the way back to the left side of the elevator. There was another door that open in the middle and it had a lever in the middle that snapped over when you pulled it, I was lucky that my fingers did not get caught in the lever when it snapped over. When the lever snapped over the outer doors to the elevator open and I had stopped between the two floors, I could see my co-workers up to their waist on the second floor, and I was able to get a little more fresh air, but I was still hot. I told my co-workers I was going to get out of this elevator, so I was hoping that the electricity did not come on while I was climbing through the one third gap that was left at the top of elevator and the bottom of the second floor. So I put my foot on the railing in the elevator and grabbed the edge of the second floor and stepped on the door lever and pulled myself through the hold with the help of a couple co-workers. I was glad the electricity did not come on again. My new directory Rhonda said Harry that was impressive how you was able to get out of there, I told her I had to adapt and overcome the situation, I was just glad the electricity did not kick in while I was climbing through the gap. I never told anybody I took a piss in the elevator! Shhhhhh! Cracking up! Bye!

The End Again!

Printed in the United States
by Baker & Taylor Publisher Services